MONSTERS ON THE LOOSE

The True Story of Three Unsolved Murders in Prohibition Era San Diego

RICHARD L. CARRICO

WildBluePress.com

MONSTERS ON THE LOOSE published by:

WILDBLUE PRESS
P.O. Box 102440
Denver, Colorado 80250

WILDBLUE PRESS is registered at the U.S. Patent and Trademark Offices.

Trade Paperback ISBN 978-1-960332-43-1
eBook ISBN 978-1-960332-44-8
Hardcover ISBN 978-1-960332-44-8

MONSTERS ON THE LOOSE

Quotes are as they appear in their sources.

TABLE OF CONTENTS

PREFACE

Three dead young women. One stabbed, one hanged, and the youngest one strangled. These are the tragically true stories of three young women, one only a child, murdered in San Diego, California, within four months of each other in 1931. They were not the only murders in San Diego that year; far from it. They were not even the only murders of women in the bayside city in the early months of 1931 or the only cases of child kidnappings. Almost daily, local newspapers carried articles documenting violence towards women of all ages. Usually perpetrated by their lovers, ex-husbands, or husbands, what would come to be known as femicide lurked not far beneath San Diego's sunny image as a beach town with quiet suburbs. Perhaps more frightening, the killer or killers in these three cases did not appear to be a family member or love interest.

A commonality of the three murders is that justice went unserved—the killings remain unsolved. But based on my research for this book, I think we could close the casebook on one murder and make some viable suggestions on another. As is often the case, all three cases lacked witnesses to the murders. Circumstantial evidence and speculation then and now are important elements of these stories and that is the basis of my effort to find justice for these three young women.

San Diego is the oldest European town on the West Coast. Its roots as a Spanish colony go back to 1769 when Father Junípero Serra and his Franciscan priests arrived. Mission

San Diego de Alcalá and the nearby Spanish *presidio* (fort) brought culture shock, violence, and sometimes death to the Indigenous Kumeyaay people. Injustices against women in San Diego go back hundreds of years. The earliest violent crimes against women in San Diego were rapes and murders of Native Kumeyaay women by Spanish soldiers; men who were rarely punished. Sadly, invisible diseases introduced by the Spanish colonists killed far, far more Native people than violent acts.

San Diego was only "Spanish" for about forty years before it morphed into a post-Mexican revolution Mexican-Californio pueblo. Remnants of pre-American San Diego can be experienced, without a great deal of authenticity, in Old Town San Diego. Then, within twenty-five years, the dusty little Mexican pueblo became the American town of San Diego. By 1931, the city of 150,000 people had become an eclectic mixture of faux-Spanish architecture, stately Victorian homes, modern California ranch houses, and the ubiquitous Southern California bungalows.

Deep canyons divided many of San Diego's streets, either cutting them off or requiring narrow bridges to span them. In Downtown San Diego, two major streets, Broadway and Market, led east/west from San Diego Bay. Broadway (previously known as D Street) served the Commercial District. Going west towards The Bay, Lower Broadway was dotted with auto dealerships, a bowling alley, shops that catered to sailors, and a variety of bars. Banks, drugstores, hotels, and high-end department stores called central Broadway home. On the far east, Broadway turned largely residential, separated by the occasional small shop. South of Broadway, Market Street hosted Chinese cafes, tattoo parlors, low-rent hotels, and small shops. South of Market had historically been San Diego's underbelly, with brothels, saloons with names like Bucket of Blood, smoke-filled card rooms, and pool halls.

On the flat mesas north of Broadway, two ribbons of concrete, running east to west, linked suburban neighborhoods with commercial districts. University Avenue traversed the undulating landscape from tony Mission Hills on the west through middle-class housing tracts, ending on the east in farmland and small ranches. El Cajon Boulevard, also known as Highway 80 along its more eastern segments, began out east in El Cajon Valley. From the flat valley floor, the boulevard ran west, gradually gaining elevation until it ran into Park Boulevard. A mixture of commercial and residential uses dotted both sides of University Avenue and El Cajon Boulevard. Before the advent of large shopping centers thirty years later, shoppers not wanting to go all the way to Downtown San Diego did their shopping along these two thoroughfares. Clothing stores, grocery stores, car dealerships, barber shops, and furniture stores served the growing populace. Reflecting the growth of automobile ownership, El Cajon Boulevard even sported a relatively new concept in dining, the drive-in restaurant.

Wedged between Broadway on the south and University several miles to the north, San Diego's founders set aside fourteen hundred acres, or about two square miles, of scrub, brushy mesa tops, and canyon land. Originally known simply as City Park, they changed the name to Balboa Park in time for the 1915 Panama-California Exposition. By 1931, most of the original buildings from the Exposition were demolished, repurposed, or consumed by fire. The faux Indian Village, near ruin in the extreme northern end of the park—which plays a major role in one of these stories—remained.

San Diego's ethnic makeup was predominately Anglo-American, or, if you prefer, white. There was, however, a sizeable Mexican population living on the fringes of American San Diego and in small barrios. Tucked away in the backcountry, the county included the largest number of

Indian reservations of any in the United States, although the total population was relatively small, as was the Black population.

Beginning in the early 1900s, San Diego gradually mutated into a navy town. With its accessible harbor, open mesas suitable for military bases and airfields, and temperate weather, San Diego increasingly drew a military presence. Not known for its industrial prowess, San Diego in the 1930s instead supported large fishing fleets, vast agricultural lands, and a burgeoning tourist industry. Brochures sent back east touted the somewhat bucolic city as the natural remedy for persons with respiratory issues and other health problems, especially tuberculosis, then known as consumption. Advertisements boasted of "perfect climate" (Lemon Grove), "miracle waters" (Spring Valley), and "invigorating saltwater baths" (Ocean Beach). The Hotel Del Coronado was on the itinerary for any middle to upper-class tourist seeking a respite from East Coast winters. Of course, the tourist brochures never mention murder or suicide.

CHAPTER ONE

MY INVESTIGATION—NINETY YEARS LATER

As an archaeologist and historian, I am well suited by my temperament and experience to investigate cold cases. Whether turning a trowel through ancient prehistoric midden soils or thumbing through pages of old historic documents, delving into the past is what I do. History itself takes on many guises. Murders, in general, and unsolved murders, in particular, are, unfortunately, one swath of the sometimes-stained cloth that is our history.

Like most major cities, San Diego has plenty of unsolved murder stories to examine. I picked the murders of these three young women—Virginia Brooks, Hazel Bradshaw, and Louise Teuber—to explore and write about for several reasons. That all three murders took place within three months of each other became a primary reason and allowed me to focus on a relatively condensed time and place. After all, I was used to viewing and explaining hundreds, if not thousands, of years of human history. Peering into a small window of time offered challenging and exciting chances for telling very specific stories.

Examining the role of sensationalist yellow journalism in the period became a second impetus. The front pages of local and national newspapers practically oozed and dripped with lurid, misogynistic headlines and stories. Newspaper reporters were not only part of the story, but they also had access to crime scenes and police investigations that today's press can only dream about. How the news was reported, and how the sometimes-alarming stories affected the public, became a story within a story. It has been said that news is the first draft of history. I would add that it is a rough draft and often rife with errors.

And finally, there were the police investigations and the unique time period itself that piqued my interest. The forensic techniques available at the time were meager but growing. The specter of past and ongoing police ineptitude, investigatory transgressions, and corruption swirled around the cases. Amidst a backdrop of the Great Depression, the Volstead Prohibition Act, and the emergence of the often-maligned "Modern Woman," the stage was set.

Ultimately, though, it was the tragic murders of three young women—one, Virginia Brooks, a child—somehow hooked me. That their murders went, and remain, unsolved and largely unexamined, almost compelled me to write about them. Their brief lives and deaths became tangible to me. What paralyzing fear these young women must have felt when the last thing they saw was their killer. Ultimately, I came to inhabit San Diego of ninety years ago. The odor of old yellowed paper, plasticky microfilm, and newsprint faded. I heard the clang of streetcar bells, I smelled the flowers on caskets, and sensed the grief for the dead girls.

But writing about the violent murders of a ten-year-old schoolgirl in February 1931, and two young women in April and May 1931, presents many challenges. The young women, Louise Teuber and Hazel Bradshaw, and the schoolgirl, Virginia Brooks, were not famous, nor rich, nor living in a major metropolis. In the ranking order of news stories, their deaths fell below those of Hollywood stars, bankers, and even mobsters.

The sensationalist newspapers of the time used evocative and emotional terms such as "bizarre," "mysterious," "fiend," "deranged killer," "poor innocent victims," and so on to describe the crimes. Unsupported speculation, rumors, and police station gossip daily filled the columns.

The press dutifully inflamed fears of a serial killer, then called a *mass murderer*. Internet and cable television did not birth misinformation; the medium of half-truths and salaciousness simply leapt from the printed page to our modern airwaves and cyberspace.

For Louise and Hazel, it seemed important for the press to describe the young women in what we would label as sexist and even misogynistic terms. Adjectives such as "stunning," "beautiful," "modern," "attractive," "well-rounded," and "pretty" preceded their names. Descriptive labels certainly not applied to young men. In the prevailing culture and, as vividly displayed in news reports, women's bodies were a battlefield and a canvas for male ideals and thoughts. Was the rationale for the detailed physical descriptions to journalistically set the stage for the reader? Or, more likely, to libidinously lure the reader into the narrative. Regardless, stirred by journalistic fervor and a sense of fear, their murders would grab local and even statewide attention for a short time and then fade back into the dark shadows of history.

At the time of the murders, San Diego supported two major papers: the morning *San Diego Union* for early risers, and the *San Diego Evening Tribune* for afternoon and evening readers, respectively. Considered a third-rate publication, the much less-read *Sun* served its own audience. The three newspapers actively and voraciously competed for scoops, advertising, and readers. Small wooden newsstands dotted downtown street corners. So-called newsboys in their flat caps, who were often older boys and even middle-aged men, hawked their wares in front of banks, cafes, and saloons. For the suburban and rural dwellers, paperboys mounted on their Schwinn bicycles flung the bound papers towards porches with admirable accuracy.

Truly sensational news coverage sold papers and the dramatic newspaper accounts of these three cases, and others, would slowly settle down. But only after the excessive and lurid coverage of the Lindbergh baby kidnapping incensed the public the following year. Reporting on criminal activities, the press, who often had a cozy relationship with the police, considered themselves part of the investigations. San Diego police officers and reporters often shared elbow room at downtown coffee shops, and surreptitiously at speakeasies south of Market Street and even in the venerable U.S. Grant Hotel (downstairs, of course, served by a private elevator).

Over nine decades is a very long time in the annals of police cold cases and criminal investigations. Documentation can be sketchy. Despite months of investigation and interrogations, police never took a suspect to trial in the Teuber or Brooks cases. There are no homicide court proceedings or judicial testimony. With or without a trial, typical documentation of the time would have included police reports, an autopsy, an inquest, maybe a hearing, and, of course, often incorrect, innuendo-filled, and lurid newspaper accounts. Newspapers, then and now, spun stories to sell papers. The truth could wait.

In each of these cases, even a California Public Records Act request, the state equivalent of the federal Freedom of Information Act, could not pry almost ninety-year-old police records open. The City of San Diego strongly asserts that police records are exempt from public disclosure under Section 2350(f) Investigatory Files, which prevents divulging information on *unclosed* cases. In this case, or cases, almost a century-old unclosed cases. Further, the police assert that for the Teuber and Brooks cases, all files and evidence were turned over to the San Diego Sheriff's Department. This reluctance to share information is, however, not unique to San Diego; reams of Los Angeles police files regarding even the infamous murder of the Black Dahlia (aka Elizabeth Short) remain locked away from the public. The San Diego Sheriff's Department was more forthcoming.

For one of our murdered women, Hazel Bradshaw, her date on the night she met her death was arrested and stood trial. That trial leaves us some interesting and revealing records to ponder, records that are public, not hidden under the cloak of "open cases files." Newspapers covered the trial daily, providing fascinating quotes and valuable insights. In other cases, even when contemporary official files and documents did exist, they sometimes got permanently lost or misplaced over the course of almost ninety years. It took over three years to track down and get the legal papers for the trial of Moss Garrison, the accused killer of Hazel Bradshaw.

My own investigative research took me to the modern glass superior court building in Downtown San Diego and to the worn-out ex-bank building in El Cajon that serves as the East County San Diego County Clerk's Office. When queried about the autopsy and inquest records for a second murder victim, young Louise Teuber, a very helpful but exasperated legal support assistant from the San Diego County Medical Examiner's Office stated, "Sorry, it appears that the actual case files went missing some time ago—we do not have the original records or even scans of them. It is nearly impossible to say what might have happened to them." Are Teuber's records an isolated case of missing files or at some point did someone in authority purposely remove the files and not return them? This poses an important stumbling block in writing these stories, and only one of many challenges.

Yet with several decades in our sometimes-cloudy historical rearview mirror, we can, at some level, know more than the press or investigators knew. Sometimes we can see patterns of behavior or lifestyles that played out several years after the cases went cold. Often, we can follow the news stories on consecutive days and tease out the inaccuracies, innuendos, and sensationalism. Maybe we can expose hastily developed conclusions, perhaps driven by a deadline looming overhead like an editorial sword of Damocles.

With the passage of time since the deaths of Brooks, Teuber, and Bradshaw, few people are alive who might remember details or specific events. We have only whispers and faded images of past events, of murder. The time gap forced me to hope that people born a little, or even years, after the murders, might have some information. In the Bradshaw murder, children made the gruesome discovery of the body. Perhaps they are still alive, or their adult children might be? Bradshaw had siblings. Could I track down a niece or nephew? Brooks was only ten years old in 1931 and had both a younger and older brother. I hoped that a relative or descendant of her brothers might have reminiscences or documents from the time. A photographer of underage girls, including one of the murder victims, had a daughter by a later second marriage.

To echo something that Bill James, the coauthor of the fine true crime book *The Man from the Train,* said, "My initial goal in writing this book morphed into becoming intimate rather than clinically historical." "By that, I mean that in the research and writing process, I truly came to know these young women and their families. It is often said that writing is a lonely process; not for me, not for this book. I frequently had the company of the three dead young women. I also grew to better understand the San Diego that existed less than three decades before I walked the same streets.

In writing these stories, I also shared an intimacy with the various settings in San Diego, not as a young woman, of course, but rather in terms of sights and sounds. The built environment and the communities themselves were familiar to me because while many structures of my youth no longer exist, I grew up in San Diego seeing many of the same storefronts, theaters, homes, and cafes that the murdered girls did. I had even walked the same smooth wood-floored halls of the old San Diego High School, the venerable Grey Castle, thirty years after Louise Teuber. Miss Referee, the daunting attendance secretary at the high school for over forty years, probably kept track of Miss Teuber's absences as precisely as she did mine, and I had a lot. I shopped at the Kress dime store where Louise Teuber worked, and I went to the movies at the Broadway theater where Hazel Bradshaw and her boyfriend Moss saw a movie the last night of her life.

Looking back on a time decades ago and getting to know the period and its people is like being the omniscient narrator in Thornton Wilder's *Our Town*. We can see the arc of history unfold and view the daily lives of the people who lived and died back then. Yet in the words of *Our Town's* deceased young Emily, about living people, "They don't understand." Emily was, of course, correct; we do not truly grasp what it was to live and die over ninety years ago. But with the benefit of hindsight, which may or may not really be 20/20, we can learn some key things about three young women who have been in their final resting place for a long, long time. We see them when they were young and vibrant—the entire world lay ahead of them, or at least it should have. Sadly, we know the end will come too soon for all three. Their flower-draped caskets appear before us, the smell of fresh earth from their graves wafting up. Sadly, we know that to this day, we hold no one accountable for their deaths. Justice may be blind, but also cold, unwritten, and unserved.

So how does one peer back through the mists of time to visualize the young women and to place their deaths in the period's context? There were several avenues of investigation; some pitted with logistical potholes, some were short, dead ends, and others led to a spider web of trails and deep rabbit holes. Just as with the murder investigations themselves, the research for this book sometimes offered hope. Often, it led to crushed theories, and occasionally, it produced a bright, meaningful substance. Occasionally, an obstacle can change into an open avenue.

For instance, being far more of an often emotionally detached historian and archaeologist than a hardened crime reporter, I had mixed emotions about contacting Diane Powe, the elderly daughter of one of the prime suspects in Louise Teuber's 1931 murder. As Donald Wolfe wrote in his superb book on the Black Dahlia murder, his innate sensitivity muted his interrogation skills and desire to pry into personal lives. But, as Wolfe did, pry and probe I did. Diane's long-deceased father, Herman Newby, a short-lived suspect in Louise's murder, spent six months in San Diego County Jail, convicted of taking and possessing nude photographs of an underage Louise. I asked myself, would the daughter who was born to a second Newby wife, in another state eight years after the murder, even know anything? If she had information or insights, would she protect her father if she had doubts about his innocence?

The actual murder aside, did Diane know of her father's conviction and jail time for taking and possessing nude photographs? Did she grow up close to her father, or were they estranged? Would telling someone about him be cathartic? When I wrote my first polite letter of inquiry to Diane, who is living in Texas, I had twinges of guilt, or at least a feeling of invading someone's privacy—and for what purpose? Well, to get a little closer to the truth, of having contact with a living person who might have insights, photos, or letters—those things form the very basis of historical research. In the Louise Teuber murder case, Diane not only offered facts and background from her own memory, but she also provided family photographs and, as we shall see, made several startling accusations.

With ten-year-old Virginia, I located a niece of the young girl murdered in 1931. Rowena Lux, the daughter of Virginia's younger brother, shared information with me. Without hesitation, she said that the murder literally tore her family apart. Something that Rowena told me about her father brought a powerful, evocative human element to the Brooks story. By contrast, the Hazel Bradshaw incident can be told only through the lens of contemporary accounts. For her, with one important exception, there can be little current narrative or documentation to fill out a more complete story.

With Hazel Bradshaw repeatedly stabbed and left behind a crumbling wall in Balboa Park, I located a nephew, Craig Bradshaw, who was reluctant to talk much about the death of his aunt. Hazel's tragic story, he said, was still well-known within the family. He told me that the family believed then, and apparently still do, that the guilty murderer got off— that a jury had erred in acquitting the prime suspect. Mr. Bradshaw seemed irritated that I would even suggest that the verdict seemed just. History itself, and not just murder cases, can possess conflicting narratives.

Mere months separated the murders of Virginia Brooks, Louise Teuber, and Hazel Bradshaw in 1931, and none of the victims found justice. Murder is, of course, a transgression, a moral dilemma that is essentially a crime against all people, against the very culture that we all share. But beyond the chronological setting and their youth, there is much, besides murder at the hands of others, that links these young women together. But realistically, why tell stories that are unresolved?

Because that is the story, the uncertainty of life and death, the often happenchance of being killed. The dark, empty void of unserved justice. All crime stories are about the search for justice and sometimes the search, no matter how well-intended, is in vain. Someone once said that all historians are, in a genuine sense, coroners—I can reluctantly accept that. And I want to give the lives of these three young women the post-mortem that they deserve.

CHAPTER TWO

THE SCHOOLGIRL WHO DID NOT MAKE IT TO CLASS

Born in Indianapolis, Indiana, as the middle child of John F. Brooks and his wife Blanche on July 10, 1920, on a sweltering humid Midwest day, Virginia Brooks would violently die shortly before her eleventh birthday. Murdered on the morning of February 11, 1931, over two thousand miles away in San Diego, California. Unlike most childhood deaths, at age ten years and seven months, a disease did not kill Virginia, nor did accidental causes; instead, a deranged murderer struck down the petite schoolgirl. Her death remains one of the oldest and saddest of unsolved cold cases in San Diego's criminal history.

At four feet six inches and seventy-five pounds, with bobbed dark hair from home haircuts, and bright blue eyes, Virginia was fairly typical of ten-year-old girls of the time. Her teachers at Euclid Elementary School in East San Diego described her as a brilliant student who loved to read. She had near-perfect attendance at school, which led to early advancement to the sixth grade. Virginia often made side trips to the public library to check out books as she walked home from school. We cannot say for sure what books Virginia might have read, but given the family's economic situation, she likely checked her books out from the public library rather than purchasing them.

Virginia may have read three books that came out in 1930, although they were not with her the day she disappeared: *The Secret of the Old Clock* and *The Hidden*

Staircase, the first and second books in the popular Nancy Drew series, and *The Yellow Knight of Oz,* a continuation of L. Frank Baum's Oz series, written after his death by Ruth Plumly Thompson, might have engrossed her. It would be eight more years until the now classic *Wizard of Oz* movie enthralled audiences. Virginia, of course, would never see that movie. We know for sure what books she had in her book bag on that February day, but more about those books later.

Friends and family said that Virginia was a quiet girl. She would rather read than play with the neighborhood children. Although some afternoons she attended Campfire Girls meetings, she seemed happiest curled up with a book or two. She had two brothers, Gordon (aged twelve), and George (aged five). The Brooks family had recently moved to San Diego from Englewood, Oregon, where John Brooks, a tall, gaunt fellow, worked as a tree feller in a logging camp. The family had moved a great deal in the past decade; Blanche Brooks gave birth to each of her three children in a different state. Blanche wore her dark hair short and sometimes severely parted on the side.

Blanche often wore unstylish utilitarian dark long dresses with lace running down the front from the neckline. Even before his daughter's disappearance, John presented a stoic appearance and a receding hairline. He often wore faded denim overalls over a work shirt and dark work trousers. Blanche worked hard to keep his work clothes clean and mended. Just because they were not well-to-do didn't mean that they couldn't be presentable.

In San Diego, John found employment as a part-time truck driver, chauffeur, and mechanic. Times were lean in the second full year of the Great Depression. The Brooks children often wore hand-me-downs from relatives in the Los Angeles area and Blanche handmade some of their clothes. Blanche appeared in line at the day-old bread counters at local bakeries, including a local favorite,

Snowflake Bread. Blanche did the Brooks family laundry by hand and pinned it with wooden clothespins to dry on cotton clotheslines strung between metal poles in the small backyard.

In February 1931, the family lived on the outskirts of San Diego at 5602 University Avenue. In the city directory for 1931, compiled in 1930, street addresses for University Avenue ends two blocks short at 5450. This shows that east of 54th, postal addresses were yet to be assigned. University Avenue was called the University Avenue Extension, showing that prior to that the paved and maintained avenue ended near 54th Street. Small houses and wooden shacks dotted the valley floor east of 54th Street. An aerial photograph of the area from 1928 reveals a few houses east of 54th Street; in fact, there are only one or two near the Brooks residence. Their small house sat at the bottom of a steep hill that rose to the north. Sage brush, buckwheat, and sumac dotted the undeveloped hillsides and canyons.

Going east or south of University Avenue, the area quickly changed to large open fields and weed-choked lots. The acreage east of Euclid Avenue and University all the way to College Boulevard remained somewhat rural. Some families kept chickens and pigs in their backyards and small vegetable gardens were common. Over on 50th and El Cajon Boulevard, McDonald's Nursery would sell you a Fuerte avocado tree for $1.35, or fresh eggs from his chicken ranch for 22.5 cents per dozen. Several lots remained empty, and near what would later be 50th and University, a large canyon angled off to the northwest. University Avenue itself is one of those streets that then, and even more so now, cuts across a diverse swath of San Diego—from upscale Mission Hills on the west, east through North Park, and then on to the village of La Mesa.

At College Boulevard, the city officially ended, and the County of San Diego assumed jurisdiction out to the western line of the City of La Mesa near Massachusetts

Boulevard. The demographics at this end of town were decidedly blue-collar and included truck drivers, cooks, military men, day laborers, and domestics. Few people in the professional class lived out here in the boondocks. The ethnic makeup was largely Caucasian, with a small enclave of Mexican families. The average rent hovered on the low end between twelve and fifteen dollars a month, compared to an average rent in San Diego of approximately twenty dollars a month. In today's dollars, fifteen dollars would be about $290. City directories for the period show families moved a great deal year to year, and such relocation grew more and more common as the Great Depression wore on. Often, a single small house would be home to two families or extended families.

If John had time to read the *San Diego Union* morning newspaper before leaving for work at around 7:15 on February 11, 1931, he would have learned that the weather forecast was for occasional rain, that critics harshly attacked President Hoover for continued inaction on economic issues, and that the aged and ailing Thomas Edison, who would die later that year, predicted that the Depression would be over within three years. Edison also opined that Italian dictator Benito Mussolini possessed great executive skills and was probably a good man for his people.

Depending on Brooks' political views, he was a registered Republican, he might or might not have expressed alarm that police in several major cities had rounded up known "Reds" for protesting in favor of what police declared to be clearly a communistic policy: unemployment insurance. San Francisco roiled with clashes between dock workers and shipping interests. The hot local issues revolved around bringing more water to growing San Diego, and whether San Diego could or should successfully annex the adjacent community of La Mesa. President Hoover declared that the United States was "fast winning over depression." John left for work a little after 7 a.m. and drove his beat-up truck down to the municipal pier. He spent most of the day hauling lath from a steamer to a lumber company.

On that overcast Wednesday morning at around 8 a.m., Virginia left the small family home on the north side of University Avenue in East San Diego to begin the approximately one-mile walk to her elementary school. It was a walk she made every school day unless she accepted a ride from a neighbor or passersby. Some mornings, a friendly real estate agent would pick her up and take her all the way to Euclid Street.

Her mother put away the crepe paper Valentine's Day cards they had been making and waved at Virginia from the kitchen window of their modest bungalow-style home. Perhaps Blanche Brooks pridefully noted how pretty her only daughter looked in her clean, starched-white dress, with the colorful flower designs, reddish-brown wide plaid jacket, and nearly new shiny black shoes. Virginia carried her lunch, which included cheese sandwiches and two oranges, in a brown paper bag, four books to return to the library—they were due that day—two Indian Head nickels in the pocket of her dress, and a bouquet for her teacher.

Walking along University Avenue to the west, Virginia's route was on what we might describe as a lonely stretch of brush-lined road. The numbered streets that crossed University got lower and lower until you arrived at 1st Street just east of Mission Hills. In the mornings and late afternoon, there could be traffic on the road and folks from neighborhoods to the east worked their way to and from jobs and schools.

At the foot of the gradual hill ascending to Euclid Street on the west, Virginia's twelve-year-old brother Gordon sped by on his bicycle and waved. Virginia laughed and waved back. On her walk, Virginia passed several vacant and run-down houses, a grocery store at 54th Street, and a gas station at 49th. At Euclid and University, if she didn't take a shortcut to the north near 50th Street, she might have noticed the Egyptian Garage with its stylized Egyptian motif façade. Since the discovery of King Tut's tomb in 1922, all things Egyptian pervaded American culture and the arts.

Several short blocks east of Euclid between 49th and 50th Street, Virginia was supposed to meet up at Winona Street with her best friend Katie Lucero to walk the last blocks to school. On the mornings when Virginia hooked a ride, she would have the motorist pull over and pick up Katie too. The previous November, Virginia and Katie played roles in a fifth-grade school play based on the Norse myth of Siegfried Brunhilda. Now, three months later, Katie impatiently waited ten minutes for Virginia, who was usually punctual. Katie's chum was not just late: she never arrived, and she never would.

Chapter Three

Gone Missing

The following day, February 12, 1931, the morning edition of the *San Diego Union* carried a small article wedged between a piece on a candy store robbery, attempts of some prisoners to escape from the San Diego Jail, and the trial of some local arsonists. Under the heading East San Diego Girl, 10, Missing, the February 12th *San Diego Union* reported that Virginia Brooks had gone missing on her way to school on the previous day. At the bottom of the article, the paper asked that anyone with information regarding the whereabouts of the girl was asked by the *Union* to "communicate with the police in East San Diego."

Thus began the often frantic, sometimes sharply focused search for little Virginia. With each passing day, the local newspapers intensified their coverage—including wild speculation and conjecture. Over the next two months, the search for Virginia shared headlines with the move to elect a "progressive" president instead of Herbert Hoover, a record snowfall in Europe, and a spike in gasoline prices, to five cents a gallon. In local news, the proposed annexation of La Mesa failed at the ballot box. Valentine's Day passed and Virginia's Euclid schoolmates opened their carefully lettered handmade poster-board hearts emblazoned with their names to find no card from Virginia.

Police work in the early 1930s bore some resemblance to current investigations but also varied in several ways. Then, as now, law enforcement agencies sometimes fought turf wars; in this case, the San Diego Police Department and the San Diego Sheriff's Department shared information but sometimes engaged in redundant and counterproductive activities. The Brooks' residence sat in a sort of no man's land between the City of San Diego and La Mesa. Being in the county, it was officially not in either city. As the newspapers noted, the sheriff's office aided the local police in the search and investigation, but acrimony popped up now and then. Both law enforcement agencies resisted any outside assistance.

Initially, the investigation of a missing person largely focuses on gumshoe detective work rather than forensic analysis. There are significant differences between detective work and forensic analysis. The former is more subjective and involves interviews and timeline reconstructions. The latter attempts to be objective and uses proven scientific analysis. This was, and is, particularly true when the person disappears outside the home because there is no sign of a struggle within a residence or building, no blood evidence, and no fingerprints to compare. Instead, investigators home in on who saw the missing person last, what the routine of the person was, and who might wish to kidnap or harm the abducted person. While probably not common knowledge at the time, eighty percent of child abductions occur within one-quarter mile of the family homes. In the case of a child, police must also assess the potential that the child ran away from home. In those cases, the missing person's home life comes under particular scrutiny. Regardless of the detective work and forensic studies, the criminalist's first duty is to the truth.

The first action in the twenty-four hours after the girl's disappearance was to interview the parents and siblings. Then, as now, family members get particular scrutiny, especially the parents. By all accounts, Virginia was a normal, happy child who had no reason to run off. Despite that, a *Union* news report dated February 14th, suggested that maybe Virginia was adventurous and took off on what they called "a hitch-hiking expedition." The next police effort was to canvas the neighborhood to both search for her and to interview neighbors and persons living along the girl's route. Local police and sheriffs began the door-to-door search for the missing girl and immediately began interviewing schoolmates, teachers, and neighbors.

Katie Lucero, who was described in the papers as the little Mexican girl and the pal Virginia was to meet and continue the walk to school with, offered conflicting stories of her activities that fateful morning. At first, she told police that she had waited for Virginia at their usual meeting place. Later, when told a neighbor had seen Katie playing near an old culvert, she recanted and said her father forbade her from playing there and she feared another whipping by him. She steadfastly denied that she sometimes played in a canyon that ran north off University Avenue and that no, she and Virginia did not go there on the morning Virginia disappeared. At one point, a local news article suggested that Katie, an adopted girl, had been the real target of the kidnapper. The supposed rationale, which was never actually explained, was that the birth parents wanted to snatch their daughter back.

From the start, the chief investigators were Blake Mason, a detective for the San Diego Sheriff's Department, and George Cooley, a detective sergeant for the East San Diego Police Department. Sheriff's Deputy Mason, aged forty-four and nearly six feet tall, presented a serious demeanor with his severely parted black hair and stoic brown eyes. With only one year of high school education, Mason was described as not overly well-spoken but a person who could strike up a conversation with almost anyone. Over the next month, Detective Mason did most of the gumshoe field work, especially out-of-town inquiries, and assisted in local interrogations. The newspapers described him as dogged and relentless.

Detective Cooley worked the local angles using his network of snitches and informants to gather information. A thirty-nine-year-old veteran of World War I, Cooley stood six foot two with coal-black hair, a ruddy complexion, and brown eyes. Officer Cooley was involved in many of the high-profile cases in San Diego over more than two decades of service. Just two years before, he helped bring to justice the killers of two money couriers from the Agua Caliente racetrack and casino in Tijuana, Mexico. Many years later, his son, George, went on to a long career as a police officer in San Diego.

The investigation continued with interviews of persons who said they saw Virginia on that fateful morning and then moved on to what law enforcement might call the usual suspects, which included known child molesters and what the March 21st *Union* labeled as "deviants and perverts." One unnamed motorist nervously admitted that he had given the little girl rides in the past but not on the day in question. The February 14th *Union* reported that he presented a strong alibi and was not a suspect.

This part of East San Diego was still semi-rural, with abandoned homes, garages, barns, and sheds that might hide the little girl. Police, concerned citizens, and even soldiers and sailors searched those places, but in vain. Blanche Brooks stressed to the officers that Virginia had always been an obedient child and certainly had not run away as some detectives seemed to insinuate. No, she told officers, there had been no arguments or friction in the family that would drive Virginia from the home. Her husband, the more subdued of the pair, quietly agreed with her on all accounts. Virginia's sad-faced brothers told detectives that they badly wanted their sister to turn up, they missed her already.

Scores of first-hand accounts of varying accuracy poured into law enforcement. Virginia was supposedly seen riding in a coupe with an older man, she was seen by a Mrs. Leah Ward talking to a man who was sitting on the dirty running board of a sedan pulled to the side of University Avenue, and she was seen playing with other children along the edge of a canyon. Deputy Mason tracked down three similar accounts in the East County where a man in a coupe was sighted driving with one hand and holding a very young girl tightly against him with the other hand.

One woman speculated Virginia might have fallen in a nearby pond. Such an accident was not out of the question; almost annually, children would drown in the sand pits of nearby Mission Valley. With that in mind, a large pond at the eastern terminus of Broadway Street in the Las Chollas District east of town was dragged, producing only old tires, parts of a stove, and other miscellaneous household debris.

For a while, the press and some detectives tried to tie Virginia's disappearance with fugitive wife killer and child abductor Everett Frank Lindsay. Lindsay had been spotted in Los Angeles, accompanied by his twelve-year-old adopted daughter, whom he allegedly kidnapped. When recaptured after an escape, Lindsay confessed to murdering his wife and burying her in the backyard, and to child molestation. But he assured the police, he had not been to San Diego and had nothing to do with Virginia's disappearance. Further investigation cleared Lindsay of any involvement in the Brooks case.

Two men from Escondido, Emery C. Odell and Charles "Bill" Williams, said they saw a little girl thirty-five miles to the north near San Marcos peering sadly out of a green coupe. Almost a month later, reinjecting themselves into the investigation, they allegedly provided a thorough description of the man driving the green coupe. The description of a green coupe interested the investigators given that a green coupe with a little girl in it had been seen earlier in the eastern community of El Cajon. To some police officers, the continued interest in a case by certain members of the public either reflects genuine empathy or the actions of a suspect. Apparently, Odell and Williams were not considered as suspects.

In his reasonably well-researched book about the Brooks case, *Abandoned Justice*, George Sherwood suggests that the two men who provided what was deemed the best description of a possible suspect may have been the killers. Although he offers little support for his hypothesis, it may have merit. Sherwood names Emery C. Odell, a furniture dealer from Escondido, and Charles Williams, a self-described trapper.

Little is known about either of these men. Odell lived in Escondido on West Grand Avenue and occasionally came down to San Diego to sell furniture and housewares. Charles Williams could be the same Charles D. Williams, a career criminal first arrested in 1917 for burglary. Williams was arrested and jailed one year after Virginia's murder. According to the *Union* and *Tribune*, the charge was "insanity to such a degree as to be a public nuisance." He was also arrested on three counts of burglary in 1941 and sent to Folsom Prison for a one- to five-year term.

Scant accurate information came out of those early interviews except that Virginia was seen walking between her home and the 4900 block of University Avenue. Most accounts agreed that she walked along the north side of the avenue on the sidewalk. The only conclusive account came from her brother, Gordon, who, between sobs, told officers that Virginia merrily waved back at him as he pedaled west on University Avenue towards Euclid.

Descriptions of the little girl, including a photo provided by her aunt, were sent to police departments and newspapers throughout the West. Law enforcement offices were yet to be tied together with teletype machines, information by telegraph passed ever so slowly. To say that the search immediately widened might be an understatement. Over a three-week period, the dauntless Detective Mason travelled more than three thousand miles by auto, investigating leads in Tacna and Quartzite, Arizona, in Phoenix, and beyond. A multitude of what appeared to be strong leads describing an older man accompanied by a little dark-haired girl poured in and Mason did his best to track them all down. On the day, February 23rd, that the *Union* and *Tribune* newspapers chronicled Mason's futile trek to Arizona, they also carried articles on a motorist burned to death in a roll-over, the shotgun killing of three convicts trying to escape prison guards, kidnappings in Chicago, and "CRAZED MEXICAN KILLS TIJUANA PATROL WAGON DRIVER." In other words, just another typical day in February 1931. Oh, and Al Capone was back in Chicago from a lengthy vacation in Florida.

On several occasions, Detective Mason, perhaps hoping to flush out the kidnapper, implied to the press that he was closing in on the culprit and his prey—maybe only a day behind their trail to the east of San Diego. By February 23rd, when Mason's superiors ordered him to return to San Diego, the search for Virginia's killer grew colder. Mason's relentless search for Virginia was not the first time he ventured far and wide in search of answers. In 1929, he and three other officers went into Baja, California, and then to the offshore South Coronado Island in search of a murder suspect. (After three weeks south of the border, his team returned to San Diego empty-handed).

Local police interviewed more than eighty persons with little to show for their efforts except wildly conflicting reports—she was seen in El Cajon, no, it was in Escondido, or perhaps with an older woman in El Centro. Police in Seattle, San Francisco, West Texas, and Los Angeles followed dead-end leads of similar versions of the story. On February 26th, hope arose when her father received a cryptic letter from a man who said he knew where Virginia was being held. The letter instructed Brooks to come to Quartzite, Arizona, and see the postmaster, who would then direct Brooks to his daughter. The unknown letter writer sternly warned Brooks not to alert the authorities. Fearful of being watched, and unhappy with the pace of the formal investigation, he complied.

Unable to simply sit at home and fret, and without notifying the police, Brooks and a couple of friends drove the two hundred forty miles to the small mining town of Quartzite on February 28th. Near the end of the more than six-hour drive, mainly on two-laned Highway 80, they crossed the Colorado River near La Paz, Arizona, and then drove the remaining twenty miles to Quartzite. Brooks talked to the postmaster at the small Quartzite post office, where he soon learned that the postal official had no idea what he was talking about.

"Heck no," he told the *Union*, he didn't know about "any kidnapped girl," although he remembered reading the sad story of Virginia in the papers. Inquiries to other townsfolk provided no information, only concerned condolences. The following day, the newspapers relayed the sad news that Mr. Brooks returned to San Diego no closer to finding his daughter than when he left.

The public read daily updates on the efforts to find the girl, and although often embellished, the news reports offered a running dialogue of the fruitless search. Front-page photographs of the Brooks family sitting on the door stoop of their residence put a human face on the tragedy. Her brothers George and Gordon were pictured mournfully looking at a family scrapbook. Informed that the Brooks family was economically strapped while John Brooks took time off work to aid in the search for Virginia and to be with Blanche, the *San Diego Union* offered a donation of ten dollars. Within less than a week, the Brooks fund had grown to over eighty dollars, nearly five thousand in today's dollars. In the press, on February 18th, Brooks publicly thanked the donors, saying, "The people of San Diego have a heart—a big heart." With all the press coverage, which included photographs of the Brooks home and their address, curiosity seekers swarmed to the neighborhood.

As part of what was heralded as the largest search for a missing person at the time, two hundred Boy Scouts combed the nearby canyons, low-flying airplanes donated by the Ryan Aeronautical Company and piloted by seasoned pilots flew over valleys and mesas. Observers said the planes flew so low that the landing gear almost scraped the taller brush. Upon landing the pilots said that they did fly as low as they could and that they needed to because of all of the rubbish strewn across the canyons. One reporter seemed to incredulously note in the February 16th *Union*, "Notable among the volunteer searchers were women. Many were women and girls who came dressed for roughing it and forcing their way through nearby growths of chapparal and sage brush." Actually, women's clubs and civic organizations played a major role in the searches. A fresh burial near Encanto caused great excitement until it turned out to be grave of a beloved neighborhood dog.

Amidst all the searches, police were called out to guard the Brooks' home after a couple in a green coupe with Kansas license plates were seen suspiciously cruising the neighborhood. A middle-aged couple even approached Virginia's aunt, named in the press only as Mrs. H.T. Moffat, and persistently asked questions about Virginia and the family. Funds continued to pour into to support the Brooks family and to fund a reward for information leading to the recovery of the little girl, or, as the newspaper grimly reported, *her body*. The reward for the capture and conviction of her abductor, sponsored by local newspapers and an anonymous donor, rose to over nine hundred dollars, including two hundred dollars from the *San Diego Union*, approximately fourteen thousand in today's dollars.

Unfortunately, by the first days of March 1931, police officials conceded that the trail had grown cold, even though as late as March 8th what was thought to be a strong sighting came in from San Francisco; that lead also proved baseless. On the one-month anniversary of Virginia's disappearance, Mr. Brooks told the *San Diego Union*, "I know she cannot be found. It is going to be hard to tell my wife that all hope is gone." A local newspaper opined on February 15th that "the figure of a fiend yesterday cast its sinister shadow across the police hunt." Throughout the search, the terms *fiend* and *monster* were writ large. The *Union* reported on February 24th that an eighty-year-old retired man, Reverend John William Greenwood, became so troubled and distraught by the Brooks murder that he jumped overboard and drowned. His daughter told police that he boarded the *Emma Alexander* for a short trip to Wilmington, climbed over a railing, and fell into the cold waters. During the ordeal, Blanche remained under the care of a doctor and her pastor, Reverend H.K. Holtzinger.

William J. Burns, of San Francisco, perhaps the most famous detective or criminologist of the era, weighed in on Virginia's disappearance and sadly agreed with John Brooks. At the time, Burns proudly wore the mantle of the Sherlock Holmes of America and had been involved in several high-profile investigations, including the Teapot Dome scandal and the bombing of the *Los Angeles Times* building. From 1921 to 1924, Burns served as the director of the Bureau of Investigation, renamed the Federal Bureau of Investigation in 1935. Parenthetically, when the FBI was established, Burns came in a close second to J. Edgar Hoover to be its first director. Supposedly, several police departments and state attorney generals did not like Burns' no-nonsense approach to investigations. Others thought he was not a team player and had expressed a view that many local police agencies were rife with corruption.

In a special interview on March 11th with the International News Service and the *San Diego Union*, Burns confidentially said that "Virginia Brooks was abducted and put to death by a degenerate moron. And he probably still is in the vicinity of his crime." In fact, Burns strongly suggested that the kidnapper lived in the immediate area and that the abduction was not happenchance.

Detective Burns based his assumptions on his interviews with the Brooks family and friends, a retracing of Virginia's last known movements, and conversations with the case detectives. Decades before the concept of profiling developed, Burns essentially worked up a profile of the kidnapper. In the same interview, Burns suggested that little Virginia "accepted a ride from a motorist, as she was in the habit of doing. Unfortunately," he said, "her 'friend' this time was a man of very low intelligence, a moron, and a degenerate." Burns speculated that Virginia was taken to a lonely shack where the degenerate abductor "worked his will upon her and killed her." Her lifeless body would, Burns stated, be found in some lonely spot around San Diego.

As investigators and the public would soon find out, William Burns was practically prescient in his reconstruction of the events since February 11th. Virginia Brooks was not traveling anywhere with anyone; she was not being held for ransom. Her distraught father and Detective Burns were sadly correct—she had been dead for several weeks.

CHAPTER FOUR

ALONE AND DEAD ON THE MESA

He could have been cured.

Nearly one month later, March 10th dawned as another cool overcast San Diego morning with temperatures in the low fifties. An overnight fog dampened hillside vegetation and streets. The morning newspaper carried an article on the upcoming inquest into the murder of young Hazel Bradshaw, found stabbed to death in Balboa Park. Other news included President Herbert Hoover's plans to build the largest air armada in world history. Then, as sudden as her disappearance, all hope of finding Virginia alive faded to black. The March 10th front page of an extra edition of the late-afternoon *San Diego Evening Tribune* blurted out, "BODY OF VIRGINIA BROOKS FOUND WRAPPED IN BURLAP ON MESA HERE." The photograph that accompanied the short news article superimposed the earlier photograph of Virginia posed between her parents sitting on the stoop of their home, an early form of Photoshop.

In sensational prose, the column head provided an abundance of detail and hyperbole: "GIRL HACKED TO PIECES BY FIEND IS DISCOVERED BY SHEEPMAN AT KEARNY." No one seemed to note the possible irony that the discovery was almost a month to the day since Virginia's disappearance. Ironically, on the day that Virginia's body was discovered, two young girls were struck and injured by an automobile at University and Euclid on the very route that Virginia would have taken. Sara A. Kropf, the driver, received a citation for reckless driving.

The article that followed the bold headline offered few details beyond the fact that George H. Moses, a self-described sheepherder, and his dog, found the girl's body stuffed into coarse barley sacks. The gunny sacks were described as old but clean. The two gunny sacks, one inside another, containing Virginia's body were found three-fourths of a mile northeast of Murphy Canyon Road and three-fourths of a mile east of what was then Camp Kearny Road. Camp Kearny itself was largely a collection of abandoned wooden barracks, weed-choked roads, and an old airfield. Prior to Charles Lindberg's epic flight to France in 1927, the Camp Kearny Airfield was where the Ryan Aeronautical Company tested the famed *Spirit of St. Louis*.

Forty-year-old Moses first lived on Menlo Street and then on Winona Street in East San Diego, less than a mile and a half from the Brooks residence. A native of New York state, he was a man of medium build, standing a little over five feet and a half, with blue eyes and light-colored hair. Moses told authorities at the time that he was a goat and sheepherder, yet his occupation on the federal census and in city directories listed him variously as a pipe corker, caulker, or laborer, but never a herder. He said he was working for a Mr. Vesay and had a little shack northward and up the canyon from his discovery of Virginia. Vesay was a local rancher with large holdings in the Kearny Mesa and Miramar Mesa areas. He and his wife lived in the small community of Miramar.

According to news accounts, Moses had been out on the lonely mesa shooting at tin cans with his pistol when his shepherd-mix dog Blackie, or Shep (the news accounts vary), became interested in a nearby gunny sack. Moses approached the sack, which lay somewhat hidden behind a mound of dirt surrounded by low brush. One account in the March 11th *Union* stated that without even opening the sack "from its position and shape Moses knew he had found a human body." Yet in a later, possibly more accurate, but still embellished account to the coroner's inquest, Moses said he slit the sack open with his hunting knife and a head rolled out. Moses told reporters that he ran to the highway, nearly three-quarters of a mile to the west and flagged down a truck. He breathlessly told the driver, "I've found a body." The truck driver drove eleven miles south to Old Town, where he found a telephone and called the sheriff's office.

Based on a map printed in the *Los Angeles Evening Express* and the description provided in the death certificate, the location of Virginia's body was between Murphy Canyon and Murray Canyon and east of what was then the San Diego-Escondido Highway, later Highway 395. Apparently, the site was less than a mile south of the goat herder's house and accessible from a rarely used dirt road off Murray Canyon.

If the killer were transporting the body from the south up Murphy Canyon Road, he would have gone past Mission Gorge and then Shepard Canyon on his right. Both canyons were occupied by ranches and homes in 1931 and would not have provided the seclusion that the area between Shepard Canyon and the Escondido Highway would have. By continuing north past Shepard Canyon and then turning northeast up the dirt road parallel to Escondido Highway, the killer could go largely unnoticed—especially if he stopped short of Moses' house.

On the other hand, if the killer were coming from the north down the Escondido Highway from the direction of Escondido, he would have turned south down Murphy Canyon Road before he got to the farms and ranches in Mission Valley, and after close to half a mile, turned to his left and gone east up the parallel canyon. With lots of secluded areas and canyons between Escondido and Poway, it would seem to make little sense to continue further down the Escondido Highway. If, however, the body had been kept for a month in the vicinity of old Camp Kearny, the approximately five-mile route south down the Escondido Highway to Murphy Canyon Road has a certain logic to it.

Law enforcement officials hastily converged on the site with news photographers and reporters close on their heels. At this point, the investigation evolved from detective work on a little girl's disappearance to a forensic investigation to determine the method of death and to collect evidence that could lead to the murderer. Officers Blake Mason, Jake Tillery, Deputy Coroner Dave Gershon, and Chief of Police Arthur Hill, with reporters and photographers dogging their every step, began their investigation of what they called the *drop site*, concluding immediately that Virginia was murdered elsewhere. Upon opening the gunny sack containing a little body, Deputy Sheriff Mason dug deep into a hip pocket. He produced a scrap of reddish-brown material with a wide plaid. Mason had carried the scrap of cloth, a part of the coat worn by Virginia Brooks when she dropped from sight, ever since he took up the hunt for her. Quietly, Mason knelt beside the mangled heap and compared the goods he carried with the coat found on the body. About him stood a circle of stern-faced men—men who did not talk. Mason was the first to speak. As quoted in the press, he said, "Virginia Brooks."

Several photographs that appeared in the March 11th *Union, Tribune,* and *Los Angeles Examiner* captured the remoteness and loneliness of the scrubby mesa. Other images show the investigators posing in their long-sleeve white shirts, dark ties, and broad-brimmed hats. Almost immediately the March 11th *Union* asserted that "ARREST NEAR IN GIRL'S DEATH." Supposedly *tell-tale* tire tracks and "clews" within the gunny sacks were offered up as important evidence. As a British criminologist noted about crime scenes, in general, many years later, the scene is the *silent witness*. Investigators certainly hoped so.

The investigators also surmised that the body had been only recently placed on the mesa, based on the newly trampled grass beneath the gunny sack, the still-fresh tire tracks in the mud, and tracks across the nearby grass. George Moses told officers that he had been in the area a few days ago and that the sack was not there then—he was sure of it because his dog would have alerted him then. That raised the question of whether the killer purposely chose the anniversary of the abduction to discard the body. A second nagging question was why the body was moved at all. The only good reason would be if the killer thought the body was about to be discovered and implicate him in the murder.

Reporters and cameramen soon gained access to the site, compromising any evidence that might have been missed. Investigation at the crime scene took several hours, far less than the days or weeks modern crime scene investigators spend. Upon hearing the tragic news, Blanche told reporters on March 11th, "I can't believe it—I can't believe it" before collapsing. Until the inquest, Blanche remained uncertain if the little body truly belonged to her daughter. Days later, Mr. and Mrs. Brooks posed for a news photographer with one of Virginia's favorite dolls. Newspaper accounts reported that Blanche appeared to still be shaken and, as the newspaper noted, she had tender recollections of her little girl but seemed "out of sorts." Armed with what he considered substantial evidence from the crime scene, San Diego Police Detective Paul Hayes boasted to the press on March 11th, "We are closing in on the killer and expect to have him in custody within 24 hours." A brash proclamation and certainly not a prophecy that would come true.

Questionable deaths in San Diego required that the deceased's body be given an autopsy by the medical examiner or coroner. Based on the autopsy, an inquest panel or jury might be convened to gather further details on the person's death. The panel could include the coroner, law enforcement officials, family members, friends of the deceased, and, if needed, witnesses. The inquest focused on determining how and when the person came to their demise, if criminal activity was involved, and finally, who might be responsible for the death. Police would then use the results to pursue a criminal investigation and if the evidence warranted such an action, recommend that the district attorney formally charge the suspect.

At the inquest, held at the Goodbody Mortuary, the Brooks family was further quizzed regarding the timeline of Virginia's disappearance, and the medical examiner and coroner made their findings known. The new, although limited, information from the inquest appeared in the press. Peering through the small pane of glass that allowed for viewing through the little white velour-covered coffin, Blanche Brooks told officials she was unsure if the remains were truly those of her daughter. To some bystanders, Blanche appeared semi-delusional.

A mortuary official opened the lid, reached into the coffin, and removed the skull of the child. As reported by the *Los Angeles Evening Express*, Blanche stared at "[t]he small collection of bones that is all which remains as the only mortal existence of the once happy schoolgirl." Reportedly, when she saw a tell-tale chipped tooth in the child's jaw, she gasped and according to the *Evening Express* said, "I have never been satisfied that my little girl was really dead. That tooth, though, convinces me of the terrible reality of the whole thing." Virginia had fallen and chipped the tooth only two weeks before her disappearance. Blanche also told the examiners that the little girl's slip, which was almost new, had been ripped and torn.

With the search and rescue operation for Virginia ended, the pursuit of her killer began. It would be a search that would cover several states and even reach Baja, California.

By the 1930s, many police investigators, at least in large cities, applied the 1904 creed of Edmond Locard, who wrote that in an abduction or murder, every contact leaves a trace. The French criminologist's phrase became known as Locard's Exchange Principal and is, of course, widely applied today, as it was in the investigation of the murder of Virginia.

To consolidate the investigation, Detective Lieutenant George Sears was placed in overall charge. Forty-six-year-old Detective Sears was a veteran officer who had led marginally successful efforts to curb vice in San Diego. Marginal because a certain amount of corruption festered within the police department and was embedded in the political system of the time. Turning a blind eye to bootlegging and sex work could be lucrative.

Sears was of medium build with gray eyes and thinning brown hair. He was well-known in the seedier parts of San Diego for his raids on speakeasies and gambling dens. In spite of his honesty and successful arrests, his critics suggested that he was not the right man to lead a murder investigation. Cuffing a man caught making bathtub gin was one thing; gathering evidence and tracking down a mysterious child murderer was another.

Literally hundreds of people were interviewed or contacted, more than twenty suspects were interrogated, and searches of countless homes and abandoned structures that might have been the murder scene were conducted. In the minds of criminologists and the lay public of the time, and perhaps still for some to this day, there existed a type of person who would do such a crime. That person would have a look that set him off from average, normal people. Phrenology or craniology, which studied cranial shapes to determine people's intellect and propensity for crime, was still in vogue in the 1930s. The Brooks investigation included the misperception of criminal types, and some men were brought in and interrogated based simply on their physical type.

Today, most criminologists discount that killers and rapists have dead eyes or other distinctive facial traits that intrinsically mark them as criminals. Yet true crime writers and television crime shows still reinforce the stereotypes going back to phrenology and the association of certain physical traits supposedly earmarking evil doers. Shifty, beady eyes, large brow ridges, swarthy appearances, and other supposed hallmarks of criminals loom large in our perceptions and vocabulary. And yet, there was Ted Bundy and others who looked shockingly normal. Perhaps we hope that the killers and deviants among us somehow look different than us, that they carry some trait that reflects their evil. We want to call them monsters and have a visceral need to separate them from the rest of humankind.

"I will leave nothing undone in this investigation and hunt for the killer!" Chief of Police Arthur Hill told the *Tribune* on March 11th, immediately after the discovery of Virginia's body. And indeed, the search was hailed at the time as the greatest ever in San Diego County. Over the next several weeks, the press, including newspapers in Los Angeles, Sacramento, Phoenix, and San Francisco, published conflicting accounts of the condition of the body and what was found in or near the gunny sacks. Some reports even suggested that some sort of acid or chemicals had been poured over the body to destroy it. That assertion was quickly debunked by the coroner and investigators.

Despite lurid descriptions in the news accounts, it does not appear that Virginia was hacked to pieces by a fiend, or even dismembered. She was not decapitated; the details provided in newspaper accounts in the beginning of their coverage suggest decapitation but back away from that description in later reports. In a reprise of the Brooks murder in 1935, the *San Diego Union* returned to reporting that Virginia had been decapitated. In more recent years, some true crime websites and blogs, in spite of more conclusive evidence to the contrary, have also erroneously repeated that Virginia was decapitated, all the better to interest their readers. Instead, the state of decomposition of Virginia's small body might have initially given the appearance of dismemberment.

Early news reports also suggested she had been disemboweled, when in fact the medical experts at the time attributed the absence of internal organs to severe decomposition and insects. The apparent lack of tearing or ripping, as would be common if coyotes or animals attacked the body, further indicated that the body had been buried or inaccessible.

Wherever the body had lain, insects or other parasites had more than a month to feed off the poor girl's body. Entomologists now know that maggots from the blowfly devour massive quantities of flesh in a matter of days. Maggots thrive on wet matter such as fresh-to-putrid flesh. After living and feeding off a carcass, within fifteen days the maggots transform into flies and leave the host. In later stages of decay and mummification, beetles feast on dry body parts. Hard-shelled beetles had taken up residency in the gunny sack.

In other words, the newspapers of the time leaned towards making the murder as fiendish and brutal as possible while producing only limited factual details. Only later did they, almost grudgingly, report on the more accurate albeit less lurid facts. In recent blogs and internet posts, amateur sleuths and true crime writers have repeated erroneous accounts of decapitation and mutilation.

Regarding the official autopsy report, which could provide more specific details, a San Diego medical examiner's official told me that Virginia Brooks' "actual case files went missing some time ago. It is nearly impossible to say what might have happened to them." In a news account at the time, Dr. F.E. Toomey, the county autopsy surgeon demurred on the cause of death, saying the body suffered extreme deterioration, but did conclude that the head had certainly not been severed from the body as the press had luridly reported. He also noted that there was no evidence of blunt force trauma on the skull or on other bones. Keep the lack of any blunt force trauma in mind, given a later accusation of guilt. General speculation on the cause of death then centered on strangulation or asphyxiation.

The death certificate itself, Number 31-016980—dated March 20, 1931—offers few details beyond stating that the verdict of the inquest jury was that the cause of death was "unknown" and that "she came to her death on or about the 11th day of February 1931 in San Diego County, California, by party or parties unknown to the jury." No mention of possible sexual assault was given at the time, although it was alluded to in newspapers and again in a 1935 news article. Most likely, a conclusive finding would have been impossible given the state of the schoolgirl's remains.

It appears that Chester D. Gunn, the autopsy surgeon who signed the death certificate on March 20th, somewhat arbitrarily assigned the date of death to the day Virginia disappeared. The document read "that she came to her death on or about the 11th day of February 1931 in San Diego County, by a party or parties unknown to the jury." Using that date may have been a formality based on the last time she was seen alive or perhaps it was to comfort the Brooks family that Virginia had not been held hostage and abused long before her death. Gunn may have been correct, as statistics on child murders suggest that almost three-quarters of children abducted by a non-family member are dead within three hours of the abduction. When her classmates at Euclid Elementary opened their red-and-white Valentine cards and munched on candy hearts, she was probably already dead.

In the 1930s and well into the 1950s, police departments held suspects for days without legal representation and routinely used strong-arm tactics to coerce confessions. Within a day of the recovery of the body, the search was initially narrowed down to three prime suspects. Those taken into custody included E.F. Morley, who had a bloody stump in his backyard, a burnt tire, and vehicle tires that seemed to match the tire tracks at the crime scene. Morley produced an iron-clad alibi and the stump, he patiently explained, was used to dispatch live chickens—a common backyard feature in some homes of the times. Morley was released without charges being filed against him.

Harry W. Wahlstrom and his elderly father lived at 3626 35th Street in what was then a rural portion of East San Diego, less than two and a half miles from the Brooks residence. They raised chickens and sold vegetables from their extensive garden that contained piles of leaves and compost. When neighbors reported that they had seen Harry furiously digging in a leaf mold pile one evening sometime after Virginia's disappearance, he automatically became a suspect. While unstated, the Wahlstrom property was probably the spot that investigators had singled out in the newspapers as a likely spot for the murder and burial. Upon further investigation of the Wahlstrom property and examination of Harry's hair, which did not match the strands discovered with Virginia, he too was released from custody.

Other likely suspects included an unnamed son of a prominent wealthy manufacturing family who was believed to harbor unhealthy attitudes towards children. As Blanche Brooks put it in a March 13th *Tribune* interview, "He has been seen in this district often and his record of degeneracy leads me to believe he might know something of the horrible fate my child met." This allegedly degenerate scion of wealth soon dropped from the newspapers as a likely suspect and apparently also from police attention.

That is until the strange disappearance and subsequent murder of Dalbert Aposhian two years later. Once again there were hints of police covering up for the sexual appetites of the son of a wealthy family. In direct conflict with the findings of Dr. Colby, Sheriff Edward Cooper asserted that Aposhian had fallen off a pier while fishing. He explained that what appeared to be genital mutilation was the result of crabs. Sheriff Cooper even went so far as to put rabbit carcasses into a tank of crabs to prove their viciousness. Colby and another autopsy official maintained that Aposhian had blunt force trauma to his head consistent with being hit and that a sharp object inflicted the boy's wounds, not carnivorous crabs. Further examination also revealed that the boy had been raped, although the word *assaulted* was used instead. The case went unresolved.

Then there was John Paul, a forty-five-year-old vegetable peddler who had served time in the San Diego Jail just the year before. He was arrested on charges related to an attack on an eleven-year-old girl whom he had lured into his home on Island Street. To escape arrest by Sheriffs Shea and Mason, Paul resisted but was captured in what the press called a "rough and tumble" fight. A neighbor girl, Rachel Munday, who lived nearby on 32nd Street, testified at his trial that she had been assaulted twice by Paul. The medical examiner confirmed the sexual assault and Paul was ultimately convicted and sentenced to one year to life. John Paul strenuously denied any involvement in the abduction and death of Virginia Brooks and had an alibi. At least the press ruefully noted one deviant, if not a murderer, was off the streets.

Very briefly, and for unstated reasons, Mrs. Helen Clough of 5065 ½ Brighton Street in Ocean Beach was caught up in the police dragnet. *The San Diego Union* declared in a March 20th headline that STARTLING EVIDENCE POINTS TO WOMAN IN BROOKS GIRL SLAYING. The article suggested that Virginia might have been tricked into getting into an automobile with a woman who served as a deviate's accomplice. In fact, earlier in the investigation, Detective

George Sears suggested that the kidnapper may have had a female accomplice. In a March 20th *Union* article, Sears cryptically added that if that was the case, "she was probably a user of narcotics." His statement reflects a common refrain from the times that many evil-doers did so under the influence of drugs. This mantra was a convenient and comforting way of separating such deviates from so-called average folk. The twenty-five-year-old married woman plaintively pleaded her innocence, as did the two Filipino male companions arrested with her. Nothing came of this lead and Mrs. Clough returned to her small white Ocean Beach cottage without being charged or further investigated.

Later, almost grudgingly, Mason and his superiors would call in professional criminologists Rex Welch and Frank Gompert from Los Angeles. In 1924, Los Angeles police developed the first true crime laboratory in the United States. In a news account, Rex Welch, a well-respected forty-year-old investigator from Los Angeles, theorized that Virginia had been strangled with the straps of her dress. He based that conjecture on the presence of knotted straps around Virginia's neck and a stick tied to the straps that would have been used to tighten the makeshift noose, or garrote. Welch makes no mention of dismemberment or disfigurement of the body, perhaps addressing only criminal forensic evidence and not physical condition.

Contrary to popular opinion, child molesters rarely kill their victims. One estimate is that less than ten percent of the victims are killed, and these murders take place because of special circumstances rarely associated with perversion or sexual gratification. The most common rationale for murder is the victim knew or could identify the perpetrator. In other instances, the child is killed by accident or to silence their terrified screams. Sadly, assuming that little Virginia accepted a ride from someone she knew, then her murder was nearly inevitable.

If Detective Welch was correct in hypothesizing that Virginia met her death by strangulation using the straps of her dress, it would appear that the abductor did not premeditate or prepare for the murder by carrying knives, clubs, or other weapons. More likely, the killer panicked, perhaps realizing that Virginia could identify him, or she may have already known him as a neighbor or family friend.

Speaking at the time on the topic of juvenile delinquency, before an audience of behaviorists and the interested public, Dr. Norman Fenton, the head of the California Bureau of Child Research, offered his scholarly opinion on Virginia's killer. The March 15th *Union* headlined his findings, "DECLARES BROOKS ATROCITY DUE TO LACK OF TRAINING." As reported in the *Union*, Fenton told his listeners, "At most only a handful of people in San Diego are capable of committing such a crime." He went on to say that clearly the killer was badly raised and in spite of what Fenton believed was a bad upbringing, the murderer "could have been cured." Dr. Fenton did not offer up what a cure might have looked like but, assumingly, it involved psychiatric therapy.

This position, of course, flew in the face of contemporary beliefs that killers and criminals were born, not made, or they were addled by narcotics and that in most cases, they were doomed to a life of crime and violence. Today, Dr. Fenton's theory is widely accepted and placing the blame on nurture, not nature, is often the basis for criminal profiling. Or, as suggested by well-known profiler John E. Douglas, maybe both nature and nurture play a role.

The basis for the development of the criminal mind aside, evidence from the discovery scene was initially thought to be of great value, but that hope soon faded. The two gunny sacks that had been telescoped over the body offered little information beyond the fact that Virginia's body had not been buried in the relatively clean sacks, and that the body had apparently decomposed outside of the bags, probably while partially buried in an earthen grave. The sacks themselves were typical of those used to store grain and could be found at virtually any feed store, ranch, and chicken farm throughout San Diego County.

The removal of Virginia's body from a possibly leaf-strewn grave and transportation to Kearny Mesa may indicate that as the hunt for Virginia intensified, the murderer feared detection of the murder scene or burial place. The risk of discovery at the kill site may have outweighed the potential for capture while moving the dead girl to a remote place. Or is it possible that the killer not only decided to move the body but also to "discover" it and lay claim to the reward money?

CHAPTER FIVE

IN HER PALE BONY HAND

As the murder investigation wore on, hope arose that the use of forensics rather than just traditional detective work would provide the clues necessary to solve the murder. The 1920s and 1930s saw rapid advances in many technologies and sciences. Human optimism for the future based on new gadgets, scientific cures, and what we would today call globalization was rampant. Perhaps a rose-colored-glasses view of the future was a hopeful bromide to treat the ills of the Great Depression.

Today, we take for granted the important role that forensic science plays in solving crimes. A long-running television series, *Forensic Files,* is based on the importance of forensic clues such as fingerprints, DNA, tire and foot tracks, and blood splatter. In fact, some prosecutors have lamented that they have a hard time convincing jurors of guilt in those cases where DNA, or fingerprints, or unique footprints are lacking. They call this the CSI effect and complain that fictional cases and even actual murders, where forensics, using the smallest of evidence, solves the crime within one or two days have jaded jurors.

In Virginia's case, leaves and leaf mold came into play. Based on the deteriorated condition of the body, or portions of the body, and leaves, sticks, and leaf mold attached to the girl's dress, the forensic specialist, Rex Welch, and other investigators, speculated that the girl had been killed elsewhere. Probably soon after her abduction. Based on the decomposition of the body, Welch also theorized that at least the upper portion of the body had been placed in either a shallow grave or perhaps within a pile of leaves or compost. As the investigation wore on, examination focused on canyons, backyard compost piles, and plant nurseries, hoping to find similar leaves and leaf mold. College botanists and plant specialists were called in to help identify the good botanical evidence and to suggest their origin.

Welch also took a special interest in the red clay and red soil found within the sack containing Virginia's body. He believed that in exhuming Virginia's body from its initial resting place, the killer had inadvertently included grave soils with the body. Welch correctly surmised that the soils around old Camp Kearny Marine Corps Base, two and a half miles to the north of the drop site contained just such red deposits. Welch thought it possible that the killer had kept the dead girl in or near one of the old abandoned barracks and may have temporarily buried her in the distinctive soil. In fact, the distinctive reddish clay is not common and has been a source of topsoil for baseball diamonds. A search of the abandoned Camp Kearny barracks and surrounding area, however, did not produce any evidence to support Welch's conjecture.

Besides the girl's body and other vegetal matter, the coarse sacks contained palm leaves, which some specialists thought might be traceable to a specific area in San Diego. Virtually all the palms used in landscaping and gardens in San Diego were, and are, non-native. Investigators hoped the palm leaves in the gunny sacks could be compared to those in and around San Diego. On March 15th, a front-page *Union* headline told readers: LEAF CLEW SPURS FIEND HUNT. Using "clew" rather than "clue" remained common especially when writers wanted to affect a pseudo-British air or exhibit journalistic flair.

For over a week, those few palm leaves seemed to hold promise for where the murder scene may have been. Investigator Welch, who had a background as a chemist, believed the leaves and the mold upon them to be relatively rare. He hoped to find the canyon or backyard where such mold might thrive. The public was told to contact investigators if they knew the source of the particular palm leaves. Welch and his team fanned out across the county, visited several likely locations, interviewed nurserymen, and collected a variety of samples. In the end, the effort at using forensic palm leaf data failed. There were simply too many palm trees in too many locations.

Nothing conclusive came from those official searches, but they spurred Schuyler Kelly, the well-experienced retired San Diego coroner, and a self-described amateur sleuth, to conduct his own search. As reported in the *Los Angeles Express* on March 23, 1931, almost two weeks after the discovery of the body, Kelly staunchly believed that he found the very spot where Virginia's body had originally been disposed of. The news article included photographs of Kelly pointing out a depression on the ground under a mature eucalyptus tree, close to several palm trees, and an adjacent pond of water. The article described the location as being three-quarters of a mile from the Brooks home and the same distance from her elementary school.

Although not stated specifically, there was a secluded canyon just east of 50th Street and north of University Avenue, remarkably close to the last sighting of Virginia. Today, the canyon still contains eucalyptus trees and palm trees that could have produced the leaves noted in investigators' notes. Although initially, in a March 23rd *Union* article, Detective Sears said, "It is highly possible it is the place where Virginia's body was left by the slayer," police investigators apparently discounted Kelly's discovery, believing they had scrutinized that canyon back in January when Virginia went missing.

Or perhaps because they did not want to admit their lack of diligence, they also were still working the lead that the red clay in one sack was from Miramar Mesa, not East San Diego. Police took forensic specialist Rex Welch to the canyon bottom delineated by Kelly, where he collected soil and floral samples. Welch's conclusion was that the soils did not match and that an animal made the depression. Kelly's speculation faded from the pages of the newspapers and from the investigation. Soon, however, he would be back in the spotlight, disputing the forensics in another case.

A second gunny sack holding the girl's books also received close scrutiny. Inside were the four books that Virginia left home with two months before. All four books were children's books, including *About Harriet,* a well-illustrated book that details the daily life of Harriet over a one-week period. A second book, *Real Story Book,* contained a compilation of timeless children's stories such as *The Three Bears* and *Peter Rabbit.* Harriet Evan Price, the artistic wife of a co-founder of the Fisher-Price toy company, did the wonderful illustrations in the *Real Story Book.* The *Real Story Book* had a glossy or glazed plastic cover with fingerprints on it. They described the prints as larger than the small hand of a ten-year-old girl. Could these fingerprints be those of her killer?

More forensic evidence presented itself in Virginia's tightly closed left hand, or as the *Union* of March 25th stated it, "in her pale bony hand." Between her thumb and palm, she clutched a few strands of hair. Rex Welch hoped to compare the hair with suspects using microscopic analyses and find a match, and thus the murderer. Welch told police detectives that adult hair differed from children's hair and that even adult hair could be differentiated from individuals. He stressed, however, the obvious—that he would need a suspect with which to do the comparison.

Even today, the use of hair itself is rarely a conclusive approach to identifying a suspect. Hair could have then, and can now, eliminate a suspect, based on hair color or thickness, or assumed ethnicity. But otherwise, until DNA and chemical analyses, hair alone offers only limited forensic evidence to take to court. In court, jurors are often told to ignore a forensic specialist who declares they have a match. Even the FBI, albeit grudgingly, has backed off on the surety of hair matches. After scrutiny, it turned out that three of the hairs matched Virginia herself, and the single unidentified hair offered scant evidence. Forensic analysis suggested only that it was probably male and darker than Virginia's. Hardly an ah-ha moment in the case.

Regardless of the hair evidence, four years later, an El Cajon rancher, Vernon Cooley, no relation to Detective George Cooley, was arrested for "mistreating two young girls." He automatically became a prime suspect in Virginia's murder. According to San Diego police, Cooley had always been on the suspect list in part because he admitted he drove down University Avenue almost every day. Perhaps more damning, some of his neighbors reported he was *peculiar*. His estranged wife of ten years, Gloria, told investigators he had warned her to not be questioned about the Brooks case.

The Sacramento Bee quoted Los Angeles forensic criminologist Frank Gompert as saying the plant specimens and parasitic mold on Cooley's palm trees were identical to those found in the gunny sacks. Upon further comparisons, Gompert then realized that the mold was more widespread and common than he initially believed. Another dead end.

Gompert reported that over the past four years, he had been carefully comparing hair samples from the Brooks case with samples from known sex offenders in the Los Angeles area. Asked to do an analysis on Cooley's hair, an exasperated Gompert said that was impossible. The Brooks evidence had inexplicably disappeared, but a search was on to find them. He said, however, that in a comparison of photographs of both sets of hair, they were strikingly similar.

Notice that even then a professional such as Gompert did not use the word *match*. Within a few days, Cooley was exonerated by the police in the Brooks case. Because of the conflicting testimony from the little girls who accused him, they also cleared him in the molestation case.

Apparently ignored, or missed early in the investigation, on March 14, 1931, a newspaper reported that items from Virginia's coat pocket were being analyzed. The contents included an orange-and-black handkerchief, two nickels wrapped in oil paper, and a scrap of bookbinding. These personal items, however, offered scant information. The only other evidence noted at the scene was a set of tire tracks on the moist earth. Photographs taken of the tracks and the tread type and tire size would be scrutinized by experts in vehicle tires. Investigation of tire treads proved difficult because of the then common practice of getting worn-out tires retreaded or capped.

The tire track evidence led to a flurry of investigations at tire shops and auto shops but to no avail. One shop operator called attention to a set of used tires that a nervous-looking man had traded for another set. Those tires were similar but did not exhibit the same wear pattern. The tire tread from the crime scene was too common and in use for several years. Again, without having the automobile of a suspect for direct comparison, the tire track by itself was of little value.

Ultimately, fingerprints from Virginia's library book cover could not be matched to those on file at the police department. Relatively small fingerprint databases beyond San Diego were not accessible. Thwarted at seemingly every turn, Welch returned to Los Angeles, where his forensic investigations aided in solving several murders before his untimely death in 1935.

An improbable piece of evidence that may or may not be related to the scene was the discovery of what an unnamed woman described as a "surgeon's glove." The woman told police she walked the crime scene out of curiosity and found the glove in the low brush nearby. That a random woman had access to the crime scene shows police saw no reason to restrict the public from the location after their initial investigation. News accounts do not state whether the glove proved to be something overlooked at the time of discovery of the body, or (more likely) a glove left behind by the investigators. They do not mention the glove in further reports, probably showing that it had, in fact, been carelessly left on the scene at the time of discovery.

Throughout the investigation, but especially in the later stages, a dark side of human nature beyond the murder itself reared its ugly head. As often happens in high-profile kidnappings and murders, crank telephone calls and letters swamped the investigators. The early 1930s saw a resurgence of interest in the occult and spiritualism. Perhaps sparking one anonymous letter writer to proclaim that Virginia was the victim of black magic and was a sacrificial object of a cultish ritual. The March 13th *Evening Tribune* could not resist printing the headline, "HINTS BROOKS GIRL 'BLACK MAGIC' SACRIFICIAL VICTIM." The letter speculated that Brooks' murder was tied to that of Nicholas Esparza, who had disappeared in early June 1927.

On September 26, 1927, Esparza's body—or more accurately, skeleton—had also been discovered near Camp Kearny, less than three miles from the location of Virginia's body. Offering shocking revelations, the March 13th letter writer cryptically wrote that, "The murder of Virginia Brooks is not the act of a degenerate man as believed. If you look for a black magic adept, seeker of a hidden treasure you will probably work on the right track." The writer said that the killer had a secret laboratory, probably is a foreigner, has associates, and uses the blood of children in his seances. The possibility of a *secret laboratory* operated by a *foreigner* using children's blood in satanic seances struck fear in the believing populace. Authorities discounted the comparison, stating that Esparza probably died of natural causes when he became lost on the mesas after playing nearby with his buddies. One medical examiner suggested that possibly the boy died from rattlesnake bites. Investigators also rejected the black magic rituals of a cult angle in both deaths.

Amidst all of this, a Los Angeles radio station breathlessly told listeners that John Brooks himself had become a prime suspect. Crank letters also suggested Brooks was actually Virginia's stepfather (not true) and therefore an automatic suspect because, as we all know, stepfathers are prone to killing their stepchildren. Tired of all the misinformation and gossip, an obviously exasperated Detective Sears called a press conference covered in the March 19th *Tribune*. Sears said all the unsubstantiated rumors "inane claptrap" of a "false and malicious" nature that hindered the investigation. Giving the murderer some credit, he said, "we must match wits with a master criminal." Sears calling the murderer a *master criminal* may have been a ploy to take some pressure off the police department. To quell the malicious rumors about John Brooks, he and his wife gave a lengthy interview proclaiming his innocence and offering a strong alibi and Virginia's birth certificate to verify her paternity.

To add to the fear, gossip, and innuendo swirling around the investigation, mysterious letters appeared on automobile windshields and under front doors, warning the occupants that their children might be next. One note discovered only a few blocks from the abduction site under the door of a gas station near 49th and University garnered special attention. The note, written in huge penciled square block letters on brown wrapping paper and signed "The Doctor," proclaimed that the letter writer had murdered Virginia. As reported in the press, he boasted it was a "PERFECT CRIME" never to be solved.

As if offended by news reports implying that the killer tortured Virginia and that the perpetrator was a sex fiend, the anonymous "Doctor" stressed that he was not a degenerate and that little Virginia had not suffered. Closing out his note, the "Doctor" mocked the police, saying that he would never be found because he was superior to the investigators. A second note, also scrawled on brown paper, was slipped under the front door of the Brooks home itself. In that letter, the "Doctor" threatened both Brooks and the police. A third letter mailed to Brooks contained accusations that the police would not reveal. Police tried to lift fingerprints off the papers that bore the cryptic missives but to no avail. The letter joined other crank correspondence in the miscellaneous evidence folders for Virginia Brooks.

A week later, on March 18th, letters signed the "Gorilla" appeared at the police department. Others were later stuck on automobile windshields. The Gorilla letter garnered large block news headlines in the March 19th *Tribune* blaring that "MURDER THREATENED IN LETTER FROM 'GORILLA.'"

In his letter, Gorilla chided the police for their inability to solve the crime and said he would kill another young girl in the following week. The Gorilla scrawled,

> I have defied your experts Ha! Ha! Another schoolgirl will disappear within a week! Let mothers and parents beware! Virginia was attacked before death and not after she died. That shows how little your experts know.

The allusion to her being attacked while alive is a reference to sexual assault. This contrasts with the letter from the "Doctor," who professed to not be a deviant. More so than the "Doctor" letters, these letters from the Gorilla struck fear in the hearts of parents and discouraged young children from walking alone to school. For days, nervous parents were seen escorting their children as they hurried to school. Attendance at some of the local elementary schools dipped. People in idling cars near schools were accosted, and strangers in neighborhoods were scrutinized and occasionally manhandled. For weeks, children could only occasionally be heard playing in East San Diego streets.

Police and parents, no doubt remembered that only three years before, Earle Leonard Nelson, aka the Gorilla Man, had been executed for a series of murders and sexual assaults. While Nelson no longer walked the streets seeking prey, there were rumors that in San Francisco and other West Coast cities, another copycat Gorilla was on the prowl. In the parlance of the times, the term *gorilla* meant a brutish man with great strength and even greater lustful desires.

The mystery of the "Doctor" was soon solved, if not that of the Gorilla. Richard Daniels, an eighteen-year-old local boy living on Laurel Street near Balboa Park with his widowed mother, was arrested for penning the so-called "Doctor" notes. Daniels told the police he and some chums just thought it would be fun to be part of the story. News accounts and documents do not show that the police formally charged Daniels or if he copped to also writing the Gorilla letters. Daniels apparently got over his teenage prank phase, attended divinity school and ultimately became the vice chancellor to Bishop Charles Buddy, the first president of the University of San Diego.

Despite interviewing literally scores of people, arresting several men who appeared to be strong suspects, and taking into custody over twenty other men labelled as perverts and degenerates, officers found nothing that panned out. The range of suspects included a local chicken farmer, a gang of teenage boys from San Diego High School, an escaped murderer from San Quentin hiding in plain sight near Del Dios, a young married woman in Ocean Beach, and several men who, after the kidnapping, were accused of committing lewd acts on children. The murder of Virginia led to a round-up and sometimes jail time for what a police lieutenant called in the March 2nd *Tribune* "all classes of degenerates." This apparently included vagrants, men with past convictions for lewd behavior, and sometimes other marginalized men. In her weekly advice column *Log From the Good Ship Life*, influential social commentator Estelle Lawton Lindsay told her readers that all such men should be summarily sterilized. Several letters to the editor heartily agreed with Lindsay, the first woman elected to the Los Angeles City Council and a socialist.

Interestingly, no mention was made of George H. Moses, the discoverer of Virginia's body, as a potential suspect or even a person of interest. This, although he found the body, which often arouses the suspicion of investigators, he owned an automobile, and at one time lived close to the Brooks family. Perhaps the fact that his hair was light colored in contrast to the dark hair found in little Virginia's fist disqualified him. Not only was Moses not a suspect, but the *San Diego Union* wrote Moses a two-hundred-dollar check as a reward for finding the body. In a photograph accompanying the notice of the reward being given to Moses by Chief of Police Arthur Hill, Moses appears uncomfortable in an ill-fitting dark jacket and wrinkled slacks. Two hundred dollars in 1931 could have bought a good used Ford or Studebaker. In today's dollars, it would equate to about twelve thousand dollars.

CHAPTER SIX

NO CROWN OF SUCCESS

On the first day of spring, Saturday, March 21, 1931, at 2 p.m. under a clear San Diego sky and a slight breeze, about four thousand persons attended the memorial and burial services for little Virginia Brooks at Rogers Mortuary on University Avenue. The building could accommodate only five hundred people within the chapel itself. Crowds milled outside, waiting for the solemn transfer of Virginia's casket to the waiting funeral hearse. Held less than a mile from Virginia's elementary school, the memorial service captivated newspaper readers. As the news reported, hardened men cried and at least two women fainted. Blanche Brooks, rarely looking up, wore a simple black dress and a sheer veil. To ensure some level of privacy, the Brooks family sat in a separate, curtained-off area.

Virginia lay in state covered by a soft white shroud within her white velour-lined casket surrounded by what reporters in the March 22nd *Union* described as "a veritable mountain of flowers." Services were led by W.A. Tenny, representing the Mormon Church of Latter-day Saints, of which Virginia was a member, and closed out by Reverend H.K. Holzinger of the Asbury Methodist Church. Virginia sometimes attended Sunday school at the Methodist Church. The *Union* reported that Reverend Holzinger assured the mourners, "It is comforting to know this little child is safe in the fold of the Shepherd's eternal care." As a standard procedure, undercover officers mingled with the crowd looking for likely suspects, but none were spotted. Police were also on hand to direct traffic and for crowd control.

The choir sang one of Virginia's favorite hymns, "Let Us Oft Sing Kind Words to One Another," a well-known Church of Latter-day Saints song. Reverend Holzinger, no doubt realizing that the police needed all the help they could get, prayed, hoping "[t]he officers seeking the doer of this deed have their efforts crowned with success." Six of Virginia's Euclid Elementary classmates, all ten-year-olds, dressed in their Sunday best, served as pallbearers, solemnly carrying the casket to the waiting hearse. Small blooms of light pink Brunner roses slipped off the casket and fell to the ground. When the services were over, a police escort of motorcycle officers accompanied the hearse to the nearby Mount Hope Cemetery. Virginia Brooks came to rest at Mount Hope in a casket donated by Mount Hope and in a plot paid for by the City of San Diego at the urging of San Diego Mayor Harry Clark.

That same day, Detective Sergeant George Sears promised *Union* readers to "rid the city of Brooks slayer types" and told the press that "[w]e must drive this type of men from the city and make the streets safe again for young children." *The Evening Tribune* of March 21st carried an article with headlines warning "WAR STARTED HERE ON DEGENERATES." Over the ensuing weeks, men labeled as deviants, vagrants, and ne'er-do-wells were rousted from flea-bag hotels, parks, and illegal campsites and driven beyond the city limits. Not to be outdone, the *Los Angeles Times* told its readers that the same effort should take place in Los Angeles. A March 12th *Times* editorial said, "A sadist or lust murderer at large is a continuing danger to every woman and child until he is put beyond the possibility of doing further harm." Speaking specifically of Virginia, the newspaper instilled further fear in the populace by suggesting that the same atrocity could befall any child. The editorial closed on a warning: "It is likely that she was picked for the victim by mere chance, and that the choice might have easily fallen upon any other child."

Three days later, Blanche and John Brooks posted a letter to the editor of the March 21st *Union*. In it, they thanked the public for their sympathy and well wishes. They wrote:

> The spirit that was apparent on all sides when we laid the broken body of our dear one in the plot so graciously given by the city of San Diego, has surrounded us at all times, giving the strength to carry on and realize that even though it was our child that was taken, the safety of many other children in homes all over the nation will be safer because of the realization that crime will be even more suppressed and principles will be raised to a higher standard. May a gracious God make up in full measure that which we can never repay.

They praised the San Diego Police Department, the sheriffs, and the investigators. They thanked the attendees at the memorial service and noted that "[t]he chapel was truly an overflowing of fragrant and beautiful blossoms. Virginia loved flowers so well." In closing, they thanked the donation of Virginia's stone marker by the Simpson Pirnie Granite Company. That same day, Coronado police arrested John Dore, a vagrant, and took him to San Diego for interrogation. After supplying an alibi, which placed him away from San Diego at the time of the kidnapping, Dore briskly left the area.

By the end of March, the murder investigation seemed at a standstill. Not so, declared Detective Sergeant Sears. At a press conference, he waved several typewritten pages, listing what he called possible suspects. Chaffing when told he really had only three likely suspects, Sears lashed out at the reporters, telling them several men were under constant surveillance. Yet, on April 7, 1931, less than two months after the disappearance of Virginia Brooks, and a little over two weeks after her burial, the *San Diego Evening Tribune* unofficially signaled the end of the investigation with the headline, "LITTLE PROSPECT OF FINDING FIEND WHO KILLED BROOKS GIRL." The press declared that "indications are now that the fiend who killed the child will go unpunished by legal means. San Diego's most horrible and shocking child murder will never be solved by police." On the streets and in their homes, many San Diegans nodded their heads in silent agreement.

Holding on to hope, in an interview with the *Union* two weeks later on March 16th, investigator Clarence Morrill asked for patience and insisted: "This type of case takes time. The Brooks crime is a puzzling one, but it will be solved, and the guilty person arrested.... I have no doubt the man who killed the little girl will be caught." A conference of the lead investigators, including Detective Sears, Sheriff Ed Cooper, and others met in mid-April to review progress on the case and to assure the public that the investigation would continue.

Authorities thought they had a break when Asher Williams of Bostonia in the eastern part of the county told investigators Hickok and Mason that he should be locked up or institutionalized because "I am unable to trust myself around young girls." He admitted to fondling at least eight girls between four and eleven years old. Williams had, in fact, escaped from a Cincinnati psychiatric institution in 1922. Further investigation revealed Williams did not own an automobile, did not know how to drive one, and was in Downtown San Diego at the time of the kidnapping. A month later, newly appointed Police Chief Percy Benbough implemented a major shakeup of the San Diego Police Department. In late April, he reassigned Detective Sears, the person most knowledgeable about the case, to a desk job. No reason was given for the transfer.

Although apparently not noted in the press on April 18, John Coberly, a local truck driver, was arrested and detained for over eight hours by Detective Sears. According to police, Coberly had told some workers that he knew something about the Brooks murder. It turned out that he was simply boasting that he read all the papers and kept up on the latest rumors about the murder. Coberly was released that evening. In October 1931, he sued Sears and others for false arrest and threatening behavior. He asserted that an officer threatened to put a noose around his neck to elicit a confession. Coberly testified the police arrested him simply to "conceal the abject failure of the police department." When heard in the Superior Court on Christmas Eve 1931, Judge Clarence Harder, a reputed friend of the police department, dismissed the suit.

Despite Clarence Morrill's earlier optimism, by early May, the press and the police had turned their attentions towards the gruesome murder of a seventeen-year-old girl, Louise Teuber, found hanging semi-nude from an oak tree at the base of Black Mountain near Santee. Two shocking murders in two months planted the seeds for theories of a deranged lone killer stalking the streets of San Diego. Some people speculated that the same person was responsible for both murders. Initially, police investigators hinted that the two murders might be related but backed off on that theory as both cases wore on. Several years later, a retrospective news article asked if it was possible that a single person was responsible for the murder of over five children during this time. Whether what we would now call a serial killer was on the loose was never truly resolved. It is certainly possible that a single person was responsible for more than one murder, especially those of children. Virginia Brooks may have been one of his victims.

John Brooks and his sons moved twice before he left Blanche in San Diego and moved to the Pacific Northwest in search of work. In a strange twist to the Virginia Brooks story, as reported in the December 10, 1934, *Union* and *Tribune*, tragedy again struck the Brooks family when on

December 9, 1934, thirty-nine-year-old Blanche Brooks died without ever learning who took the life of her little girl. In the San Diego County Hospital, Blanche died from what the coroner reported on her death certificate as a "self-induced abortion" leading to peritonitis. At the time, abortion had been banned in California for slightly more than three decades. In medical jargon at the time of her death, "self-induced" could mean that Blanche had in fact tried to abort a fetus on her own. Or that she was unwilling to name the person who performed the illegal abortion.

At the time of her death, her husband John had been working for several months in Portland, Oregon. It is uncertain if he had gone there to seek work in the logging camps or if he and Blanche were separated for other reasons. Under what circumstances Blanche became pregnant and by whom remains, like so much of the Virginia Brooks story, unknown. As if hoping for a dramatic deathbed confession or some other new piece of information, Deputy Coroner Boyd B. Moran aggressively interviewed Blanche as she went in and out of a coma. He told reporters for both the *Union* and *Tribune* that he pressed her to divulge if she had "failed to tell officers anything" important to the kidnapping and murder of her daughter. If Blanche did know more, and I doubt it, she would take her grief and secrets to the grave.

Out-of-town family members buried Blanche Brooks near her daughter at Mount Hope Cemetery on December 12, 1934. The headstone reads MOTHER, rather than WIFE AND MOTHER, perhaps indicating that her side of the family made the burial arrangements rather than her husband. John Brooks, living in Leavenworth, Washington, remarried in September 1935, nine months after the death of Blanche. His two sons, Gordon and George, lived with him and his new wife. For most people, the Virginia Brooks tragedy faded into recent history.

End of story? Well, not quite. In 1935, Detective George H. Brereton assumed the position of deputy sheriff and lead criminal detective under newly appointed Sheriff Ernest Dort. Brereton possessed excellent credentials, having studied under renowned criminologist August Vollmer at the University of California-Berkeley. He worked in law enforcement in the Berkeley and Santa Cruz areas before coming to San Diego. Brereton was a powerful advocate for fingerprinting all criminals and for sharing that information widely. Sheriff Dort assigned Brereton to investigate cold murder cases, especially that of Virginia Brooks. At several points between March and July 1935, the press obliquely reported that Brereton had interrogated several men who were good suspects. Brereton dismissed the report, saying that some reporter must have been having a "pipe dream." During his investigation, Brereton took samples of Vernon Cooley's hair. Reports in the July 26, 1935, *Union* simply stated that his hair appeared of the "type" and was similar to one of those hairs clutched by Virginia.

Throughout 1936, Brereton, working with criminologist Frank Gompert of Los Angeles, pursued several leads pertinent to the Virginia Brooks case, including one child murderer in Fresno and one in Sacramento. Hearing that a serial killer with the unlikely alias of Slipton Fell and the improbable but real name of Ralph Jerome von Braun Selz was being held in San Francisco for the investigation of at least two murders, Brereton's interest was piqued. His interest grew when he learned that Selz may have lived in San Diego at the time of several unsolved murders, including Virginia Brooks. Deputy Brereton traveled to San Francisco, where he interrogated Selz.

According to one account in the *Union*, he asked him about the murders of Brooks and young Louise Teuber, whose unsettling story is in the next chapter. Selz mockingly answered, "I know all about that. Well, maybe I did and maybe I didn't." Unable to pin Selz down on the San Diego murders, police tried and convicted him on the murder of Ada French Rice, the ex-wife of the mayor of Nome,

Alaska. In March 1936, Selz received a life sentence to San Quentin.

Over fifteen years after the disappearance of Virginia, a sailor, Dennis Dent Stroud, told police he knew for a fact who killed the little girl. The *Union* for February 2, 1946, reported that Stroud told investigators that a one-time bootlegger, while drinking with him in March 1931, told Stroud that "[Virginia] attempted to cross the road and I was driving along in my truck, I hit her and put her in my truck."

While at his house at 4276 Altadena Avenue, the bootlegger, Owen Jack Hayes, allegedly further explained to Stroud that he kept the body for a while at the very house where they were drinking. A police check of military records showed Stroud had, in fact, been in San Diego at the time of Virginia's murder. Acting on this new and startling information, District Attorney Thomas Whelan immediately issued a murder complaint against Hayes, who was living in Sacramento.

Shocked at hearing he was a suspect in a murder, Hayes turned himself in to the Sacramento police. They summarily brought him to San Diego. Yes, he admitted, he and his wife (now ex-wife) Anna lived in San Diego only a few blocks from Euclid School at the time of Virginia's disappearance, and he certainly remembered the tragic murder. Hayes, who was sixty-five when interrogated, told DA Whelan that at the time of Virginia's disappearance, police interviewed him and, with his full permission, Boy Scouts combed his home, including his basement.

Whelan and police interrogators pressured and cajoled Hayes for over fourteen hours, but Hayes steadfastly maintained his innocence. The February 2nd *Tribune* noted Hayes wore a brightly colored lumberjack shirt, wrinkled blue slacks, and an old leather jacket, Hayes, near exhaustion at one point, blurted out to the DA, "I don't know anything about that child, Tom Whelan!"

Hayes' ex-wife Anna told reporters and the police that any thought or suggestion that Owen would accidentally kill a child and then hide the body and move it to avoid discovery was ridiculous. She made it clear that nothing of the kind happened in her home. Anna told officers that they were both sad for the unfortunate Brooks family. Hayes offered an alibi for the day of the kidnapping, telling police that he was out in El Centro delivering illegal Canadian whiskey to some prominent customers. He said he was not sure, however, if they would vouch for him given the nature of their business with him.

On February 6th, the *Tribune* reported that the police wanted all charges against Hayes dropped. DA Thomas Whelan refused to cancel an upcoming hearing and railed against the police for backing out. On February 26, 1946, Hayes' accuser Dennis Stroud underwent further police interrogation but steadfastly refused to testify under oath. In an off-the-record narrative, this time the story changed, and he claimed Hayes took the body to Kearny Mesa right after the tragic accident. A buddy, Tony Cito, whom Stroud said could verify Hayes' confession back in 1931, claimed to not know of that event—only that he and Stroud and Hayes talked about the murder—but then, as he said, who didn't at the time; it was a big deal.

A police review of the fifteen-year-old coroner's report that made no record of broken bones or skeletal trauma that might show a collision with a vehicle further weakened Stroud's story. After almost two months of interviews and interrogations, DA Whelan refiled the ongoing case as unsolved and instead brought charges against Stroud for making false and misleading statements to law enforcement. In a contrite admission of his lies, Stroud said he had hoped to receive the supposed large reward of fifty thousand dollars that he heard of through scuttlebutt. In fact, by 1946, no active reward was being proffered. On March 31, 1946, Whelan turned Stroud over to naval authorities at Long Beach, where the disgraced chief boatswain mate faced military justice. But for Virginia Brooks, there would never be justice.

In 2005, the Brooks case made the news again when the San Diego Sheriff's Department received a federal grant to open and try to resolve cold cases by using DNA. They assigned county cold cases to sheriff's homicide expert Curt Goldberg. Although Goldberg did not reopen or investigate the Brooks case citing an assumed lack of DNA, he examined the Dalbert Aposhian murder. The investigative team under Goldberg essentially overturned the homicide ruling from the 1930s and determined the cause of Aposhian's death was accidental drowning.

CHAPTER SEVEN

DEATH OF A "MODERN GIRL": LOUISE TEUBER

Just before noon on Sunday, April 19, 1931, twenty-nine-year-old Antonio Espinoza Martinez, from rural Lemon Grove, pulled off the winding concrete ribbon known as Mission Gorge Road. He parked his automobile in a flat area at the base of Black Mountain within what is now Mission Trails Regional Park. The coastal marine layer of fog had burned off, and the temperature was edging towards the high sixties. Martinez was a day laborer for a lemon packing association in National City. Born in Mexicali, Baja, California, Antonio lived in a neighborhood described as having a "Mexican population with no paved streets or addresses."

In the early 1930s, northern Lemon Grove, where Antonio lived with his wife and two sons, was relatively remote from urban San Diego. Getting away for an afternoon picnic broke up the monotony of rural life in the barrio. The Espinozas picked up their mail from a nearby post office. Home delivery was years in the future. In fact, city directories of the time that list the community of Lemon Grove do not list the more than forty-five Mexican families who lived there, despite Mr. Martinez and others appearing in the 1930 federal census.

During the day, the wooded area, which included huge oak canopies, was a local picnic spot for families. Boy Scouts and urban hikers known as the Sunset Hikers often hiked the nearby canyons. Before Mission Gorge Road was rerouted and widened, the old two-lane concrete road linked the farms and ranches in Mission Valley with the communities of Lakeside and Santee. The road was a major corridor, winding its way along the San Diego River. Automobiles and trucks traveling down the road made a distinct sound as their tires passed over the roadway seams.

In the evenings, however, the oak canopy hosted a different clientele—a younger party crowd drawing on unfiltered cigarettes and toasting with illegal liquor. As one local rancher who drove cattle through the valley ruefully called the get-togethers, they were "petting parties." A few years earlier San Diego State College (now San Diego State University) began the ritual of marking the upper hillside of Black Mountain with a large white *S*. Initially formed by clearing brush and applying lime and whitewash to the ground and granodiorite boulders, the *S* became more permanent when a local paint store donated gallons of white paint to the college. Large rocks were collected and formed in an *S* shape. For decades, the controversial symbol became a landmark. Some years the glowing light from road flares held by college fraternity boys at night illuminated the *S*. Over time, Black Mountain, also known as Cowles Mountain, also came to be known as S Mountain.

Martinez, his wife Margaret, and their two young boys walked a few yards towards a favorite picnic spot and the shade of old oaks. Along the well-used path, they were careful to avoid patches of poison oak. Perhaps they caught a whiff of the pungent white sage growing nearby. Spring rains filled the San Diego River, which could be heard passing over current-slicked rocks to the west. If Martinez carried a newspaper with him, the investigation of the murder of little Virginia Brooks was still news. A deadly earthquake had struck Russia, and devastating oil well fires in Oklahoma were raging.

Before Martinez could unload the wicker picnic basket from his vehicle, he made a gruesome discovery, one that he later said he never forgot. Amongst the gnarled oak trees and leafy ground cover on the canyon floor was a nearly nude young woman hanging by a rope from a tree limb. The dusty shoes on her feet barely scraping the ground. Hurrying his family away from the scene, Martinez drove to the nearest payphone and contacted the La Mesa chief of police, C.H. Mercer, who called Chester Gunn, the San Diego County coroner. As reported in the April 20th *San Diego Tribune*, the sad saga of the death of seventeen-year-old Louise Teuber had begun.

Being a teenager has probably always been tough—at least in modern times and particularly in American culture. At just a few months over seventeen years of age, Louise Teuber represented a new generation of young American women; they grew into young adulthood during both Prohibition times and the first years of the Great Depression in the 1930s. Teenagers were wedged between the so-called flapper jazz age and World War II. In 1931, Herbert Hoover was their president, and on the East Coast, Franklin Roosevelt served as governor of New York. Newspapers of the time carried stories that might sound familiar today: President Hoover said the economy needed a little boost but was overall healthy—perhaps a copper tariff would help. Real estate was a volatile market and six percent interest home loans were available yet, given a national unemployment rate of almost sixteen percent, few people in San Diego, or elsewhere, could afford to purchase a home.

Then, as now, the scandals and divorces of Hollywood stars regularly made the front page. Economically driven suicides were on the rise, as were murder-suicides. Local newspaper editorials warned of mindless radio shows and corrupt politicians. Fanned by nativist groups, including the KKK, there was growing uncertainty about how many immigrants the United States could absorb. Southern California entered negotiations to guarantee a water allotment from the Colorado River—locals feared a drought. Soon, the newspapers would carry the story of the gruesome death of Louise Teuber.

The young men and women of the era had more free time and independence than the previous generations did. In part because of the automobile, the younger generation was far more mobile than their mothers or older sisters had been. Perhaps too mobile for some tastes, given that the University of Illinois, for example, as reported in the April 21st *Tribune*, banned autos from campus to reduce what they called "heavy necking and petting." Locally, police patrols made it a habit to cruise slowly in their black-and-whites past cars parked in so-called lovers' lanes near Balboa Park, Presidio Park, and Mount Helix.

In more than one news article, Louise was called a "Modern Girl," which could mean several things to different people. To the older generation, it might mean slightly immoral or loose, too overtly sexual, or flippant. A *Sacramento Bee* newspaper cartoon, the often-satirical *Aunt Het* series in the *Union*, showed a matronly older woman in the foreground and a sleek, short-haired young woman in the background. The caption read, "When I was a girl a dress had to pinned on, but a modern girl just holds her dress above her head an' wiggles an' she's ready to go." An ad for a new movie entitled *Illicit* depicted a young woman in a provocative pose with the tagline of "Exposes a Modern Girl's Adventures in Stolen Love." For the younger set, Joan Crawford and Barbara Stanwyck were the epitome of the Modern Girl. Their movie roles played that theme, and their adventurous lifestyle embodied it. And staying on movies, one jaded pundit said, "The modern girl isn't affected by the movies. They go in one eye and out the other."

To younger people, it could denote what was later called cool or hip. A Modern Girl was, depending on class and ethnicity, prone to be flashy, often quite fashionable, and used more lipstick and cosmetics than her mothers and grandmothers. Sometimes rebelling against the male-dominated world, she might reject the role of dutiful daughter, projecting an ancient form of modern femininity. Employment outside the home was one hallmark of a Modern Girl and the wages she earned promoted independence and fostered consumerism. Lucy Jenkins, the dean of women at Boston University, told an audience that being a modern girl meant that she "should be able to solve her own problems." A Bayer aspirin ad suggested they could use a little help. The ad featured an attractive young woman with short hair and makeup and proclaimed, "no modern girl needs 'time out' for the time of month." Louise and her cohorts exhibited their modernity in sexual, economic, and political ways.

Perhaps as a sign of her liberation, and mimicking many female movie roles, Louise Teuber occasionally smoked cigarettes. Louise might have smoked unfiltered Camels, which just introduced a new form of packaging—cellophane-wrapped packs to ensure freshness. Or perhaps she lit up a Lucky Strike, for which one newspaper ad featuring a well-coiffured young woman quoted as saying she sought purity in her smokes because "my cigarette does touch my lips and is a personal, intimate thing with me." And after all, what could be wrong with lighting up? Doctors, portrayed in their white medical garb, touted the healthful benefits of smoking in full-page advertisements. Lighting three cigarettes from a single flaming match was, however, believed to be bad luck, not the act of smoking itself.

Popular culture of 1931 included the release of the movie *Dracula*, the adoption of the *Star-Spangled Banner* as the national anthem, and swing music gradually replaced New Orleans jazz, which had shoved waltzes and polkas aside a decade before. More and more homes, at least in the middle-class and above, had radios with their large dials and glowing glass tubes. In San Diego, KFSD AM 600 was the most popular with *Amos 'n' Andy* in the early evening, Paul Whiteman's band a little later, and dance music from 10:45 p.m. until signing off at midnight. A lot further up the dial, KGB 1330 carried what they advertised as harmonies, Hawaiian melodies, and dance music. Sports fans tuned to KFWM 950 out of Hollywood where they could catch minor-league baseball games, including the Hollywood Stars, who would become the San Diego Padres five years later.

Dance music and the emerging big band sounds of Cab Calloway and Duke Ellington cascaded from radio speakers. These incredibly talented Black musicians might be welcome in American homes as disembodied troubadours on the airwaves. But if they came to San Diego to play a gig, so-called Black Codes barred them from staying at white hotels like the U.S. Grant. Instead, they played at the Creole Palace and stayed at the adjoining Douglas Hotel on Market Street downtown. Both well-known establishments were co-owned by a Black business owner. South of the border in Tijuana, they played for audiences in mixed-race venues and stayed in the best hotels, including at the luxurious Hotel Agua Caliente.

The top songs of 1931 reflected the eclectic mix that became American music of the times. Cab Calloway had "Minnie the Moocher," which contained coded lyrics to drug use that included muggles, pre-Harry Potter slang for marijuana, and reference to someone being a coker. Duke Ellington had "Mood Indigo." There were several Latin-themed songs, including the "Cuban Love Song." Fred Waring and Bing Crosby both charted with "I Found a Million Dollar Baby (in a Five and Ten Cent Store)." Perhaps young Louise Teuber identified with that song given that she indeed worked in a five-and-dime store.

Born in 1914 in San Diego to Elenore and William Teuber, Louise was only two and a half years old when her mother suddenly died. As a teenager, Louise Teuber wore her dark hair just above the shoulders in a short bob that was the style of the time. Film star Louise Brooks, who actually filmed a couple of her silent movies in San Diego County, had popularized the style.

In her San Diego High School yearbook photograph from 1930, Louise Teuber presents the image of a happy young woman with an engaging smile and vivid eyes. In fact, her nickname was "The Happy Kid." In a photo taken only a year later, where she sports lipstick and makeup, she looks older and more glamorous. There would be no more photos of Louise alive after April 1931.

In the time's lingo, Louise hung out with her *gang*, meaning a group of friends that formed a social clique. Louise had attended San Diego High School, but after some unnamed issues, they sent her across Park Boulevard to Snyder Continuation School, also known at the time as the Part-Time High School. A probable cause of her being "sent across the street," as Snyder was known, might have been her poor grades. In her last semester at San Diego High, she failed English, received a POOR grade in bookkeeping, and was only AVERAGE in typing. Perhaps the change of venue did her good. Louise excelled at the continuation school and two months before her death made the Snyder honor roll in January 1931. The last entry on Louise's final San Diego City Schools Census Card stoically, and perhaps callously noted "Deceased (Murdered)."

Louise casually dated several young men, and her close circle of friends included former high school classmates, co-workers, sailors, and family friends. They went roller skating at the Mission Beach Rink, attended dances at various ballrooms that dotted the landscape, spent idle time at the beach, and went to the movies at the ornate Mission Theater. In her diary, Louise noted she saw *Sit Tight*, a musical comedy starring Joe E. Brown and Winnie Lightner. Her gaggle of friends also occasionally drove up an unmarked dirt road off of Mission Gorge Road to a secluded party spot in an oak grove. The grove sat at the foot of what was then Black Mountain, now known as Cowles Mountain.

Myretta Farris, barely able to speak through her sobs, later told investigators she was one of Louise's best friends. They were roughly the same age and attended high school together. Myretta, nicknamed Mamie, lived on the edge of Downtown San Diego in the Stockton neighborhood five blocks south of Market Street. Myretta worked with Louise at the Kress Five & Dime store on Fifth Street and hoped to save up enough to go to college. Louise had less scholastic goals. She simply yearned to get out of boring old San Diego. Myretta and Louise frequently met up to go roller skating at the Mission Beach Roller Rink or to the movies, especially the new talkies that then thrived in San Diego. Because it was in the neighborhood, they frequented the North Park Theater on University Avenue near 30th Street.

A young man who attended San Diego High School a year or two before Louise, Leslie Airhart excelled at the 440-yard run on the same track team as Bert Ritchey. Ritchey, an all-star Black athlete, later became a San Diego police officer and then a well-respected attorney. Airhart was blond, five ten, one hundred sixty pounds, with blue eyes. Leslie lived on Arizona Street, a few blocks south of University Avenue, just over a mile from Louise. After high school graduation, Airhart worked at the San Diego Soda Works and then at Consolidated Aircraft, a precursor to General Dynamics, and palled around with Louise and her friends. Leslie and Louise were good friends, and although they dated, it was only for a brief time.

A handsome, blue-eyed pilot friend of Louise, Cyril L. Smith, took her on flights around San Diego from the airfield at what is now Lindbergh Field. Louise wrote in her diary that Smith was "awful nice." In 1931, the year of Louise's murder, Cyril was twenty years old and had attained the status of flight instructor when he was nineteen.

He flew gamblers and other players out of San Diego down to the Agua Caliente racetrack in Tijuana. Some of his close friends also alleged that there might have been a bottle or two of hooch flown back across the border.

As quoted in the April 20th *Tribune*, Smith said of Louise that "Miss Teuber had more dates than any girl he ever knew." Smith lived with his mother a little more than half a mile from Louise on Florida Street just north of University Avenue, near her father's barbershop. In later years, he worked as a welder, mechanic, and during and after World War II as an aeronautics instructor.

In conversations with her friends, Louise sometimes liked to embellish her stories and maybe even create boyfriends or fiancés who did not exist. On the Friday night before her death, she supposedly told Lillian Dusenberry, a close friend, that she and a new boyfriend were eloping the next day, bound for Chicago. Uncharacteristically, Louise would not divulge her suitor's name or provide other details. There was some speculation that the mystery boyfriend, if he existed at all, was a Jerry Tallman, whom Louise had introduced to a newsboy pal a few days before her death. Little was ever known or learned about "Jerry," although Airhart had also mentioned him to investigators.

Louise and her widower father William and her grandmother lived on Vermont Street just to the north of a deep canyon that separated their neighborhood from Hillcrest to the southwest. The Teubers lived in a slightly-above-middle-class neighborhood with average rent close to the thirty dollars per month mark, which was the rent that Mr. Teuber paid. The average annual wage hovered right around $1,850 or nearly ninety cents an hour. As an experienced barber with his own shop, William Teuber probably made, with tips, a little more than that. Louise covered some of her own costs with her eleven dollar per week salary. She sometimes ditched school to pick up extra hours at the store.

Mr. Teuber owned a radio set, as did many of his neighbors, who worked as art teachers, managers, truck drivers, or owned small business owners including hair salons, barber shops, and a meat market. Situated a few blocks from the more affluent Hillcrest neighborhood, Teuber's neighbors included families from Northern California and the Midwest, with a sprinkling of immigrants from England and Sweden. People rarely locked their doors, although after the murder of Virginia Brooks, they kept a closer eye on their children.

Louise and her father increasingly argued over her lifestyle and nightlife. He thought his daughter spent too much time out of the house and ran with some kids that he did not approve of. Perhaps he even agreed with some editorials that decried roller skating as too sexual and permissive, what with all the touching and those short skate skirts. He was quoted as saying that yes, Louise was a Modern Girl, but that she was "clean" and not a bad girl at all.

But as teenagers tend to do, Louise sought her own independence. Not only was San Diego stifling, but her home life was also too confining. In a letter written to her father and delivered only after her death and then published in the April 25th *Tribune,* Louise penned, "Dear Dad-I have tried for a long time to be satisfied with the way you are running the house and I can stand it no longer. I am leaving home to-night and I am not coming back." Sadly, prescient words.

Louise felt smothered in San Diego and, despite having plenty of friends and activities, longed for a more adventurous life. She left her sister a note that, according to the April 21st *Tribune*, said in part, "When you get this note, tell the folks not to worry. I couldn't stay in San Diego another day…" At the bottom of the note was a childishly drawn skull and crossbones. In a letter to her aunt and uncle in Chicago, written the week before her murder, she apologized for not writing lately, but she wrote, "I was just a little girl trying to get along. Everything comes at once and I don't know which to do." She told them she went roller skating a lot and was getting pretty good at what she called "fancy skating" and could even do backwards turns. She also complained that "[t]his town is so dead I am afraid it will burn up some day. No excitement at all."

She closed by saying, "Gee, I want to come back to see you, but I don't know, maybe I will or won't. It all depends." They offered her a place to stay and help in finding a job, but only if her father agreed. Mr. Teuber had agreed with Louise that when she turned eighteen, she could go to Chicago. At home, she dearly loved her grandmother but chaffed when the older women criticized her makeup (too much), her dresses (too short), and her smoking habit (disgusting).

Chapter Eight

Nearly Nude, Hanging from an Oak Tree

On Saturday morning, April 18th, amidst a coastal fog barely reaching a few miles inland, Louise left her house on Vermont Street just north of Washington Street to go to work in the hardware department at Kress' dime store in Downtown San Diego. She walked the couple of blocks south to University Avenue, where she caught the Number 11th streetcar to Fifth Avenue. At Fifth, she transferred to another streetcar that took her downtown to her job. A couple of nights before, she and her father had quarreled again over her late nights away from home. Later, William Teuber came to regret his harsh last words with his daughter.

While later accounts of her movements in the last hours of her young life are conflicting, a general pattern emerges. In the workday's course, several friends dropped by the store to say hello. Some saw her on breaks and shared a cigarette with her, and others were her co-workers. She told Edwin Spencer, a friend and taxi driver, that she was going to go to Seattle that evening. There was no mention of a new boyfriend, a fiancé, or an elopement to Chicago. He made plans to meet with her at 5:30 to talk more about her plans. Louise did not show up as planned.

Louise had drawn her weekly pay of $11.65 in cash, securely sealed in its small manila envelope, from her friend and Kress' cashier, Dore Sena, around 5:30 that evening. Sena told detectives later that Louise quit her job that afternoon and hoped to leave for Chicago that night, not

Seattle, as she had told Spencer. Maybe to see her maternal grandparents. These ambiguities in what Louise told people befuddled investigators. What was true and what sprung from her lively, seventeen-year-old imagination remained uncertain.

Several people met up with Louise downtown after dark around 6 p.m. and she was in good spirits. Louise went shopping for some undergarments at the nearby National Dollar Store. Her friends, of course, did not know they would never again see Louise alive. What fatal journey took her fifteen miles away from Downtown San Diego to that lonely valley floor in Mission Gorge?

The police examinations and legal efforts that followed the discovery of Louise Teuber's body reflect the best and worst of criminal investigations. At the crime scene, investigators took several photos of the hanging body and the surroundings. Evidence was carefully noted and collected, including a twenty-foot length of heavy, carefully knotted rope, Louise's neatly piled clothing, a brown army blanket, and other personal items, including the wristwatch still on her cold, limp wrist. Her purse, which contained no money despite her drawing her weekly pay in cash the day before, turned up days later, three hundred yards south of the body. Investigators speculated it had been thrown from a car.

It is uncertain if the police sealed off the crime scene for more than just that Sunday morning so they could return for more clues if needed. Probably not, and once the murder made the Monday morning newspapers, curiosity seekers no doubt swarmed the place. A passerby may have found the discarded purse and opportunistically taken what petty cash it contained. Losers, weepers, and all of that.

Taken to the medical examiner's office, Louise's body received an autopsy and post-mortem evaluation. Given the detailed published accounts, the local newspapers clearly had access to police and sheriff's informants, and to the crime scene. In fact, the extant rather graphic photographs of the crime scene are from the *Union-Tribune* archives. Over the coming days immediately following the murder, the press carelessly careened between printing lurid details, rumors, and wildly conflicting "facts."

In their own misogynistic way, the press practiced a literary form of public victim shaming and objectification. Police revealed the contents of her leather-bound diary, with gold bindings and a small padlock to guard its secrets. Those secrets turned into salacious fodder. Various newspapers from San Diego to Sacramento labeled Louise the "Butterfly Girl," the "Party Girl," the "Five and Dime Girl;" her diary "revealed a love of a good time," "fun times with lots of fellows." Louise was "17 and pretty," she was the "attractive 17-year-old store clerk," she was "the pretty young store clerk," "pretty young shop girl." While not explicit, the coded message might have been those attractive "vivacious" young women, "Modern Women," who liked a "good time" might meet bad ends. Bad ends brought on by their own actions.

The press ignored the passages about making Easter dinner for her family, that she sadly noted the birthday of her late mother, the night she cancelled a date to be with her ill grandmother, or the nights she stayed home and read. Or her reflections on how much her sister Isabel and Isabel's husband Joe were wild about each other. They also ignored the letters to her aunt, where she proudly wrote that in the past year, she had only missed a week of work and that was only because she was terribly sick with an awful cold. Sometimes there is a gray zone between victimology, where one studies a victim's history to understand probable motive, and profiling the victim as somehow inducing their death.

Because the inquest documents for Louise are apparently lost or misfiled, I have had to rely on the newspaper reports more than I would have liked. Teasing out the truth from misinformation provides valuable and interesting details. By the time the autopsy report was filed, the newspapers had settled down somewhat and probably gave a reasonably accurate account of the inquest and subsequent events.

On the death certificate, dated April 27, 1931, the place of death is listed as three-quarters of a mile from Black Mountain. Actually, the oak grove was a bit more than a mile to the northwest. The area fell within La Mesa and County of San Diego jurisdiction, resulting in the sheriff's department leading much of the investigation. The semi-secluded canyons and oak-cloaked valleys around the edge of Black Mountain were well known among young people as places to party, make out, and, occasionally, drink prohibited alcohol. According to friends, including Leslie Airhart, Louise had attended at least one gathering there six months before, a Halloween party in 1930. Some said she often went there in the early evening after work, around 6:30 p.m., with unnamed boyfriends. Perhaps it was one of her admirers who carved a *T* or an *L* in a nearby oak as reported by the May 1st *Tribune*.

Her pilot friend, Cyril Smith, told an acquaintance that Louise frequented the oak grove. Smith was taken into custody by police on the front stoop of his mother's home and interrogated at length. His somewhat vague alibi for the evening of the murder was that he was alone at the swings in Balboa Park. Authorities released Smith, and he apparently was not considered a prime suspect or person of interest.

More than twenty years later, while driving on old Mission Gorge Road towards Santee, Smith left the main road and traveled down a dirt road to the murder site. Pulling over to the edge of an oak grove, Smith pointed out to a student of his exactly where the hanging was. He bragged that he had sexual relations with Louise. As related to me in a telephone interview with Smith's passenger, Thomas Jordan, Smith told him in a matter-of-fact manner that Louise choked to death before she was hanged. That statement agrees with various newspaper reports about the inquest and autopsy. Officially, however, the exact manner or cause of death appeared on the official death certificate dated April 28, 1931, as "hanging by neck," Smith told Jordan that he knew the actual cause; Louise choked to death while performing oral sex. Not only that, but Smith also took Jordan to the exact tree where she died. A bit shocked by the new information, I asked ninety-three-year-old Jordan if Smith told him who the murderer was. Jordan said Smith told him he did not know. Nor did Smith divulge how he knew the specifics of Louise's death.

In his testimony, Leslie Airhart told the inquest panel that on the Friday night two days before her death, Louise tried to borrow money from him for her upcoming trip. He refused her. At the same inquest, Myretta Farris mentioned she had seen an army blanket similar to the one found near Louise's body in Leslie Airhart's automobile. All eyes turned to Airhart, who quickly explained that his blanket was a gray navy blanket, although he did occasionally borrow two army blankets from his sisters. He was sure that they could produce their blankets for the investigators. To his relief, the police found his sisters' blankets and believed Airhart's alibi. He was dropped from the list of suspects and persons-of-interest list.

A more promising suspect, at least at first, was Harold Duncan. The twenty-seven-year-old part-time taxi driver had briefly dated Louise and is probably the "D" mentioned in her diary as having house parties. The evening of the discovery of her body, Duncan had attempted suicide by swallowing arsenic or some other toxic chemical. Found wandering downtown streets, he was detained and placed in a psychiatric ward for observation. When interrogated, he admitted he had dated Louise but usually only in the sense that they attended the same house parties. He volunteered that for sure he palled around with what he called "the

Kress girls." His excuse for taking the pills was economic despondency and a feeling of hopelessness, not the tragic death of Louise. His alibi checked out, but they kept him on a watchlist of possibly deranged persons.

At some point, someone unnamed hired a private investigator who turned up an interesting lead. One of Louise's friends mentioned a slightly older guy that Louise had met at the "Part-Time High School." He seemed interested in Louise but did not hang out with the regular gang. In a diary entry for February 3rd, and quoted in the April 25th *Tribune*, Louise wrote, "Came after me and we went to night school. It rained and we had a keen time." The "night school" was Snyder Continuation School, also known as the Part-Time High School. Police determined the guy was Robert Casey and went in search of this new person of interest. A tipster said Casey was holed up at the Central Hotel on Sixth Street downtown. Known as a cheap lodging house for transients (rooms went for two dollars and fifty cents and up, with housekeeping an extra dollar) most tenants stayed only a week or so.

A search of Casey's room produced a pile of magazines and books on mysterious murders. Of more interest to the police, they found handwritten notes on how to make a murder appear to be a suicide. The cops noted it looked like Casey had left in a hurry on April 8th, a week and a half before Louise's murder. One lodger suggested Casey was going to join the military under an assumed name. Changing identities in the 1930s was far simpler than it is now. No other details were provided on the search for the interesting Mr. Casey.

The police reported that when last seen downtown and prior to her death, Louise wore a "sport outfit" comprising a light blue silk skirt, a white silk blouse, hose, and undergarments. On her otherwise nude dead body, she still wore gunmetal-tinted hose rolled down five inches from her knees and dusty, dark leather shoes. As reported, Louise's clothing was neatly piled at the murder scene, leading some investigators to surmise either that the scene was staged to emulate a suicide or that she willingly removed her clothes (except for her silk stockings and shoes) perhaps to prepare for a photoshoot or some other activity. A parcel nearby contained a newly purchased brassiere and hose with a receipt.

Moving beyond details of clothing and general location, the autopsy report attempted to resolve speculation about whether the young woman had died by suicide or been murdered. Investigators initially developed the suicide angle, certainly not her friends or family. Astonishingly, in the 1920s and 1930s, San Diego sadly ranked in the top two cities for recorded suicides with a rate of fifty per one hundred thousand. For comparison today, according to the Department of Public Health, suicide rates hover between thirteen and sixteen per one hundred thousand. Several of the San Diego suicides, but a minority, were of young women who were recently jilted, pregnant, or in an unsatisfactory home life.

The rare, but not unknown, occurrences of women dying by suicide in the nude, however, especially by hanging, are often discounted by police investigators. For example, the family, some investigators, and many profilers seriously doubted the findings in the 2011 Rebecca Zahau case in Coronado, California. In that case, a young woman was determined by authorities to have hanged herself in the nude off a small balcony. While still unresolved in the minds of many people, the Zahau family won a civil suit against the brother of Rebecca's lover.

Homicide detectives pointed out that Louise must have been taken to the lonely spot, given that there was no evidence that she drove herself. Yet no cabbies remembered taking her there. The circumstances of the rope, in terms of positioning, did not show that she had lifted herself up from the ground. Someone had carefully tied the end of the rope to an adjacent tree or large bush, probably after she had been hoisted aloft, which further discredited death by suicide. And, while never conclusive given that suicidal, distraught people sometimes hide their true feelings, her friends said that she did not appear despondent or unhappy. Just bored with San Diego, not with life. They reported Louise was in good spirits and looking forward to leaving town. She was last seen downtown around seven o'clock, getting into a dark sedan.

Unlike the Coronado Zahau case, Chester Gunn, the county coroner, quickly eliminated suicide as the cause of Louise's death. Based on the autopsy surgeon, Dr. F.E. Toomey's report dated April 28, 1931, he concluded that Miss Teuber suffered at least two blows to the back of her head, was choked, and then hanged. The report further suggested that Louise was strangled or gagged, but not to death, before she was hanged. This is indicated by the "collapse of the lungs, absence of air in the lungs, and dried and swollen tongue." Her neck was not broken by hanging, further indicating she had strangled to death. Dr. Toomey concluded Miss Teuber died from strangulation, although her hyoid bone was intact. In most strangulation deaths, the relatively fragile hyoid bone is fractured or broken.

According to that scenario, her killer had hit and strangled her, probably in a fit of rage, before putting the noose around her neck and hanging her. Existing records do not suggest that Louise choked to death from forceful oral sex, as reported later by Cyril Smith. It is uncertain if the autopsy included an examination of her mouth or throat. A pre-mortem bruise on her left hip showed that she had fallen or been slammed to the ground on that side. Some investigators surmised from the position of her body in rigor mortis that someone had actually killed her elsewhere and then taken her to Mission Gorge. Once there, a suicide scene was created.

Possible specks of human skin under her nails implied Louise put up a vain struggle before her death. Remnants of only partially digested egg and bread in her stomach gave investigators some clue as to her last meal no more than twelve hours, and probably more likely less than four hours, before her death. No alcohol, drugs, or signs of poisoning showed up in Louise's blood or stomach.

The examiner reported that two wounds or bruises were present behind her right ear and at the hairline. He speculated that Louise was hit from behind. The wounds were likely inflicted by a heavy ring of the type worn by men. Perhaps from a military-style ring, which ex-military officers often wore for years after their retirement. Without using the word *sexual*, which was a little too risqué, the autopsy reported that there was no evidence of "assault." A finding of assault would have been based on examination of her vaginal or anal area and not, perhaps, her mouth or throat. The cause of death inked on the April 28, 1931 certificate of death reads, "Ascertain, Hanging by neck by partyes or party unknown."

At the inquest held on April 27th, Louise's father William sobbed before he collapsed and had to be consoled by family and onlookers. From his later testimony, he felt overwhelming guilt for not keeping track of his daughter and for fighting with her the week of her death. The last time he had seen his daughter was the Thursday night before her death when they argued about her late-night hours, and he restricted her to the house. They were close, but Louise told friends that "Pops just doesn't understand me."

On Tuesday, April 28th, last rites for Louise Teuber drew friends and family to the Merkley Mortuary in Hillcrest. Banks of flowers surrounded the casket, many placed there by Louise's coworkers and friends. Her father requested the rites should be private. They honored his request within the chapel, but outside, crowds gathered. He had purposely selected the Merkley Mortuary because it was where the last rites for his wife were performed fourteen years before. William Teuber softly cried as undercover police detectives scanned the mourners, hoping the murderer might be in attendance and reveal some signs of guilt. The April 29th *Union* reported that Reverend Milo Atkinson oversaw the services and asked for divine guidance "that officers might seek out the slayers." Following the service, Miss Teuber was cremated. Her ashes were then buried at Greenwood Memorial Park near the remains of her mother.

Perhaps because of memories associated with his murdered daughter, Mr. Teuber moved from the Vermont Street address a few blocks over to Robinson Street shortly after the funeral services. Tragically, two years later, while on a cross-country trip to visit relatives in Chicago, he died in his broken-down auto near Perry, Oklahoma. According to authorities there, Teuber apparently tried to crank his disabled auto, felt faint, crawled into the back seat, and died. The cause of death was heat exhaustion. Neither father nor daughter made it to Chicago to see their relatives.

Photographs

Ten-Year-Old Virginia Brooks. (San Diego Union 1931).

William J. Burns. America's "Sherlock Holmes." (California State Library).

Officer Mike Shea points to the spot where the body of Virginia Brooks was discovered. The officer to his left is O. C. Macumber who later worked on the Louise Teuber case. George Moses, discoverer of the body, is to Shea's right holding his .22 rifle. Moses' dog, Blackie is in the center. (Los Angles Evening Express 1931).

Investigators studying tire tracks at the Brooks'
"Drop Site." (San Diego History Center/
Union Tribune Photo Archives).

John and Blanche Brooks posing with one of
Virginia Virginia's favorite dolls after discovery of
the dead girl's body. (San Diego Union 1931).

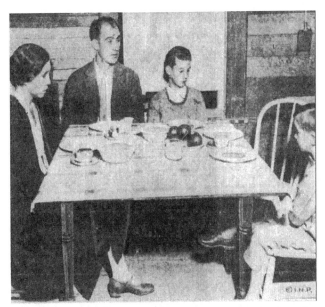

A clearly staged photograph of the Brooks family
that appeared in the San Francisco Examiner on
March 12, 1931. The evocative caption read,
"The Vacant Chair." (San Diego Union).

San Diego High School yearbook photograph
of Louise Teuber. (San Diego Union/San
Diego High School Alumni Association).

Louise Teuber posed near 900 West Broadway in downtown San Diego the year before her murder. (San Diego History Center/Union Tribune Photo Archives).

Louise Teuber left her home on Vermont Street and never returned. (San Diego History Center/Union Tribune Photo Archives).

Hanged from Tree

Coroner's surgeons at San Diego, Cal., announced an autopsy on the body of Louise Teuber (above), pretty 17-year-old girl, whose body was found hanging from a tree near La Mesa, had revealed evidence that a struggle preceded the girl's death. It was indicated the girl was either dead or dying when her slayer placed the noose about her neck and pulled her body to the limb of the tree.

Louise Teuber as she appeared in some newspaper articles. Dead at seventeen in a manner most gruesome. (San Diego History Center/Union Tribune Photo Archives).

Coroner and police at the Louise Teuber
murder site April 19, 1931. (San Diego History
Center/Union Tribune Photo Archives).

Detective Mason displaying the Teuber murder rope, her
diary on the right, and her clothing. (San Diego Union).

Herman Newby U. S. N with unnamed sailor
in the foreground. (Diane Powe).

Supreme Court Judge Arthur Munro Presiding.
Judge Munro found Herman Newby guilty of
possession of indecent photographs of Louise
Teuber. (San Diego City Clerk's Office).

Pals Richard Roehl and Jess Zimmerman posing at the
Hazel Bradshaw murder site. (San Diego Union).

Hazel Bradshaw. Death by vicious
stabbing. (San Diego Union).

The Hazel Bradshaw murder scene. The investigators in the center of the picture are pointing downwards towards where Hazel's body was found. Note the two boys in the right center. They are Richard and Jess, the boys who discovered the body. ((San Diego History Center/Union Tribune Photo Archives).

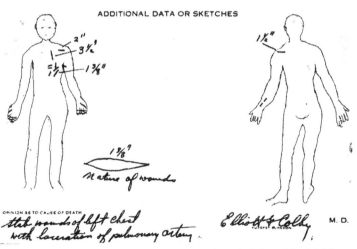

Hazel Bradshaw autopsy report sketch May 10, 1931. (San Diego County Medical Examiner's Office).

The faux Indian village in Balboa Park in 1918.
Thirteen years later Hazel Bradshaw's body was
found just beyond the low wall behind the dancers.
(San Diego Public Library Postcard Collection).

Moss Garrison. The indicted suspect in Hazel
Bradshaw's murder. (San Diego Union).

CHAPTER NINE

THE "UNUSUAL SNAPSHOTS"

With the finding of the autopsy and inquest becoming official, and death by suicide discounted, authorities began investigating the death of Louise Teuber as a homicide. As with most such investigations, the immediate family usually heads the list of suspects, followed by lovers or close friends, persons with known motives, and finally strangers, or at least persons unknown to the victim's family and friends. William Teuber was never seriously considered as a suspect.

In retrospect and using profiler techniques, the killer probably was a large or at least physically able white man, age somewhat indeterminate but likely between twenty-five and forty-five years of age, who held a low opinion of women, and given to occasional fits of rage. He probably owned an automobile, had experience tying half-hitch knots in relatively thick rope, was what professional profiler Robert Ressler recently labelled an organized killer, and, assuming that she had not been kidnapped, although that is possible, knew Louise well. For profiler Robert Ressler, an organized killer is one who is methodical, neat, and highly functional. One man in particular, as we shall see, fits this profile well.

The body offered important information regarding her likely death struggle, including the wounds to her head, and even the dust on her shoes. They took fingernail scrapings from the victim but without a suspect to compare them to and lacking the DNA analysis of today, the bits of possible, but uncertain, human skin were of little value. Investigators assumed, however, that the killer might have scratches on his face and arms. Yet even that was uncertain, given that the county chemist did not determine if the scrapings revealed human tissue or human blood.

Remnants of an egg sandwich in her stomach led detectives to canvas late-night diners to see if anyone remembered serving her. That she may have eaten after last being seen at around seven o'clock seemed like a good clue. A server at an all-night diner on Imperial Avenue in Encanto told of making an egg sandwich for a sailor who then took it out to a young woman waiting in a running car. Again, what looked to be a strong lead failed to pan out.

Investigators pored over Louise's diary found in her belongings at home. They hoped to find clues to her inner thoughts and recent movements. It surprised them to discover that her entries stopped on April 10th, more than a week before her murder. There was some sign that several pages had been removed—perhaps by Louise to hide some activity or a person's name? Even within the diary, she would sometimes refer to a date as *D* or *the boy*.

Beyond providing several names of friends and places she frequented, the diary offered little to further the investigation. The press, of course, labeled the diary as the musings of "good time girl." In other words, the musings of a young woman who had too many boyfriends, too many dates, and one too many late-night assignations.

At first, a layer of reddish dust on Louise's shoes seemed to have been picked up while she was roller skating—perhaps revealing her actions between 7 p.m. Saturday night and her murder. Yet none of her friends reported skating with her that evening, and interviews with employees at local rinks, where she was well known, turned out negative. Later, forensic analysis showed that the dust was more likely from the short walk from a vehicle to the death spot along a dusty dirt trail coated with reddish soil. Or, as some later suggested, being pulled across the soil. Red smudges discovered on the carefully knotted noose proved only to be rouge or lipstick from the victim.

The hanging rope, with its precisely tied double-hitch noose, became a major focus, with assertions that whoever tied the knot knew what he was doing and likely had navy or at least nautical experience. P.E. McCaffrey, a well-known ship's chandler, examined the rope and declared that only a professional sailor could have woven the eye splice found on the rope. Investigators also surmised that whoever pulled the rope from his position beneath the oak limb to hoist Louise's probably unconscious approximately one hundred twenty-pound body possessed significant strength to do so.

The oak tree limb bore abrasion marks attesting to rope sliding on its surface as Louise slowly ascended to nearly, but not quite, clear the ground. Then the killer tied the loose end of the rope to a nearby shrub, walked to his car, and drove off into the night. In his reconstruction of the murder, Lieutenant Sheriff Ed Cooper told reporters for the April 22nd *Tribune*, that "after placing the noose about her neck and seeing her ivory-white body against a black background... he probably became frightened and left in a hurry." Obviously pure speculation, but not an unlikely scenario either.

Reports of the exact type of rope initially varied from that used to moor a small boat to a dock or a thick hammock rope of the type used on naval ships. Forensic analysis showed that the rope had never been submerged in salt water. Several rope specialists claimed it was not a nautical rope at all, but of the type used by riggers and construction crews.

In mid-May, investigators thought they had traced the rope to the Silver Gate Cab Company, where it had been used to tow disabled vehicles. Clerks in stores that carried that type of rope were questioned, but the rope was not new and could have been purchased just about anywhere in the past. As with all leads regarding the origin of the rope and its owner, that trail, too, quickly went cold. In the 1930s, it was not unusual for the trunks of autos to contain sturdy ropes, shovels, loose boards, and other implements used to tow disabled vehicles or to dig them out of ruts on the many unpaved roads of San Diego. Once considered a major clue, the rope became just another piece of interesting evidence.

At first, it seemed as if the tire tracks from the murder scene might yield important and damning information, just as similar clues initially provided hope in the Virginia Brooks case. *The San Diego Union* offered some insight when it headlined "AUTO TIRE CLEW GIVES NEW LIFE TO SEARCH FOR TEUBER SLAYER." Using the best forensic methods of the time, the tracks were photographed and sketched. It is, however, uncertain if they made plaster casts, as would be the case today. With the cooperation of local tire shops and auto dealerships, they compared the photos to tires sold and used in San Diego.

A consensus arose that the vehicle using such tires might have been a Model T-type automobile with relatively thin tires and not a truck or heavier vehicle. A motorist who testified he passed by the murder scene around 1:30 a.m. on Sunday morning spotted a man and a car along the dirt road off the main paved road. According to the witness, the hulking man approached his auto in a somewhat confrontational manner, as if resenting the intrusion. The passerby quickly sped off. Given the moonless night, all he could provide investigators with was a general description of the automobile. Probably an older model, he guessed.

At least one witness stated that Louise left Downtown San Diego that Saturday night with a man in a late model Ford Model T touring car or similar vehicle. That type of vehicle would have been consistent with the type of tire tread at the crime scene. They discontinued Model Ts in

1927, but it remained the most popular automobile on the road. Narrowing down possible vehicles at the murder scene proved difficult. After a flurry of news reports that the tire impressions led to new suspects, the investigators admitted that, after all, they could derive nothing of substance from the tire evidence. It was useless unless they cuffed a suspect and analyzed his car and his tires.

In the search for the murderer or potential connections to the murderer, the rumor mill ground out innuendo, half-truths, and the occasional accurate detail. In her wake, Louise left a wave of both fictional and fanciful stories about her love life and her plans. At least one acquaintance, Loretta Othick, told investigators that Louise secretly married a fellow in the navy. Othick said she had inadvertently seen a ring in Louise's purse and her friend confessed she was married. Another friend was fairly sure the supposed secret husband served in the marines. But not positive, she said. After hours of interrogation, a sailor on the USS West Virginia, supposedly married to Louise, proved to be neither married to her nor a viable suspect. This despite a newspaper's misleading headlines, "REVEALS SLAIN GIRL MARRIED" and "FRIEND CONFIRMS REPORT TEUBER GIRL WAS WED."

Louise's older married sister Isabel Prouty, a stenographer, debunked such notions and said she would have known of any such arrangement and told the Union on April 22nd that Louise "was having too good of a time to get married." Exhaustive investigation did not turn up a secret husband or even a fiancé.

It was rumored by her sister and a close girlfriend that Louise had engaged in a brief romance with an older married man. He, too, was never identified. Other persons of interest included a young man who falsely confessed to achieve notoriety, a couple of local sex offenders, and as was the case earlier with Virginia Brooks, what might be called the usual suspects. A middle-aged man described by coworkers as creepy had hung around Kress' trying to induce the young women into joining what he called a dramatic club. Some of the Kress girls described his club as a cult. He seemed, they said, particularly interested in Louise. Suspiciously, there had been no sightings of the stranger since they found Louise hanged.

A suspect who briefly flitted across the investigation scene appeared to be a good possibility for the murderer, given circumstantial evidence and certain events. To this day, he may remain a viable candidate to be Louise's murderer. Little is known about John Parcellano (also spelled Parcellana) beyond the fact that within days of Louise's murder, he hanged himself in a San Mateo, California, cemetery. Parcellano's tenuous link to the murder was his method of suicide using what was described as a similar noose. He also had scratches and bruises on his face, and he may have been in San Diego when Louise died. As much as the police wanted to pin the murder on someone, anyone, Parcellano temporarily moved to the top of a shrinking list of suspects. Yet, even knowing that dead men tell no tales, without clear ties to Louise, the police ultimately exonerated the unfortunate Mr. Parcellano.

Less than a week after Parcellano's suicide, a man approached Thomas St. John, who worked at the Park Manor Hotel on Fifth and Spruce and asked where he could mail a letter. St. John said the hotel had a mail drop and he would be glad to post the letter. But as he walked into the lobby to use the mail slot, St. John noticed it was addressed to the San Diego Police Department and the coroner's office. Instead of posting the letter, St. John gave the letter to the desk clerk and alerted police, who immediately sent a patrolman to take custody of the document.

The letter, without stating who the police thought the suspect was and offering no solid evidence, warned them they were pursuing the wrong man. The writer said that Louise's killer was indeed the deceased John Parcellano.

Investigators alternated between believing the letter was from a crank, or perhaps was an actual effort to divert their attention from some unspecified suspect. Police insiders even speculated that the writer knew someone in the department and that person leaked sensitive information. The investigators gave little or no credence to the accusation against Parcellano. The mysterious letter was never again alluded to in the investigation. Who the letter writer was and his connection to the murder remains unknown. It is unlikely that the man was the actual murderer, so he may have been just a crank, or someone paid by the murderer to post the letter. Given his inquiry about where he could post the letter, he may have been from outside the area.

The canvassing of Louise's many friends continued. All the young men Louise knew spoke well of her, and the investigation did not turn up anyone with any animosity towards her. Police established that she dated several young men, and her girlfriends supplied the authorities with a list of guys to investigate. Apparently, there were no jilted lovers or disgruntled ex-beaus, or at least none came to light.

One early suspect, however, suddenly piqued the interest of law enforcement and set off alarms with the local newspapers. The phrase "unusual snapshots taken near some back-country mountain resort" appeared in the April 21st *Union* early in the investigation. At first, the papers cryptically reported only that police knew the identity of the photographer. He was being sought for questioning. Soon, the name Herman Newby came forth.

The *Union* and *Tribune* both reported a search of amateur photographer Newby's home produced "numerous wood nymphs, paintings and copies of classical art paintings, based on living girl models and on photographs." Claiming to be an artist, Newby proclaimed his innocence of violating moral codes. On April 22, Herman R. Newby, a neighbor of the Teuber family, was arrested and jailed on possible morals charges involving young Louise Teuber. His wife, Cecile, posted a five-hundred-dollar bond that evening. They released him to await formal charges and trial.

Herman Russell Newby was born on March 6, 1891, in Hancock County, Indiana, to Nellie Russell Gapin and William Robert Newby. Nellie and William had three children together, with Herman being the middle child. According to his daughter Diane, Herman angrily maintained that his mother had sexual relations with a Black neighbor, although as she noted, he used a more common derogatory term for the unnamed man. When drunk, which was far too often, Herman raged he came from that illicit coupling. This misconception, later disproved by DNA conducted by Diane, may have been one root of the vitriolic disdain that Herman developed towards women.

Nine years after Herman's birth in 1891, Nellie and William Robert Newby appear in the 1900 federal census as living in the small community of Center, close to fifty-five miles northeast of Indianapolis, Indiana. They list William on the census as a laborer and there are three children in the household on East Main Street: Grace, fourteen years of age; Raymond, seven years old; and Herman, aged nine.

The marriage of Nellie and William did not last and by 1907, Nellie had married a younger man, Francis N. Brown, an employee of the railroad, in Marion, Indiana. With the marriage of Nellie and Francis, Herman, aged sixteen years, gained a stepfather. Francis was a good father and husband, but Herman wanted to see the world. One year later, in May 1908, Herman, who apparently had little formal schooling, joined the US Navy at seventeen. His military records show he had a lanky frame, large hands, and stood just a little above six feet tall.

A skilled wood and metal worker, Herman became a carpenter on the *USS Huntington* and served on that vessel during the early years of World War I. His tour of duty included several trips to South America and into the watery war zones off of England and France, where the ship took part in submarine hunting. During this time, he wrote a series of postcards to a woman who lived in Indianapolis, Indiana. In a strange coincidence, in 1912, the navy stationed Newby on the *USS West Virginia*, the same ship that one of Louise's supposed suitors served on nineteen years later.

The postcards, which depicted photos of Herman on the front, were mailed to Myrtle Eberwuk and contained often self-effacing chitchat on the back. Copies of the postcards were provided to me by an anonymous family member. Referencing his postcard photograph, Newby wrote, "This is a poor likeness of my really ugly mug. Please do not pass judgement on this." On one postcard, Newby cryptically wrote, "Coming events cast their shadows before." And signed the card "A bum shadow." The *coming events* quote may be from a famous painting by Charles Caleb Ward with that title, or from an 1859 novel by Conway Kieta. Or maybe a reference to a well-used phrase dating back decades.

In later years, Herman served on several ships rising to the rank of lieutenant junior grade. In December 1921, after thirteen years in the navy, Newby retired because of some type of unstated disability. By nature, he was quiet and reserved unless he was drinking, which was frequently, when he would turn violent. With his penetrating grey eyes, pronounced brow ridges, and a somewhat flattened nose, Newby's face seemed to shift from placid to livid, from stoic to intensely threatening.

A year before Newby left the navy, he married a young woman named Cecile May Pease, and moved to San Diego sometime a little later. Both Cecile, known as Ceci, and her parents, had been living in San Diego for some time. An accomplished craftsman who fancied himself an artist, Newby began taking classes at the San Diego Academy of Arts in Balboa Park, where he honed his skills as a photographer and painter. Early in the marriage, Ceci worked as a milliner in nearby La Mesa. She took part in local arts and crafts fairs and was well known in the small community.

An interesting newspaper account from August 1922 reported that H.R. Newby, a well-known ex-navy man, completed an amazing and fast cross-country truck trek. The article noted he had made the 1,815-mile trip from Wabash, Indiana, to San Diego in a Service Red Pyramid truck in record time for a solo driver. He averaged 21.6 miles per hour and got 14.4 miles per gallon. The driving stunt was to advertise the trucks, which were manufactured in Wabash, and which Newby hoped to sell or rent from the General Garage on India Street in Downtown San Diego.

The Newbys purchased a small bungalow on Maryland Street in a quiet community on the edge of University Heights a few miles north of the San Diego Zoo. They also had access to her parents' small cabin in the mountains east of San Diego. The enclave, known as Whispering Pines, near Julian was sparsely occupied and usually only seasonally. Those San Diegans who could afford it spent leisure time in the summers at mountain cabins, air conditioning in San Diego being uncommon. For Newby, part of the attraction of Whispering Pines may also have been a small group of nudists who frequented there. According to his daughter, her father always wanted to be a nudist. Embarrassing her, he often paraded around their small house in the nude.

In retirement, Herman Newby had a hobby that brought him great pleasure but also would send him to jail. He photographed nude or semi-nude young women and then either retouched the enlarged photos or painted portraits from the photographs. Over eighty years later, his daughter Diane would explain that her father used some sort of device that allowed him to trace or transfer the small photographic images to larger canvases. Once there, he would then paint them in oils. According to her, her father did not sell the paintings. He gave some as gifts to family members, but most he kept for his own enjoyment. Diane said that her father took his art seriously and considered himself a creative artist. As he would explain his collection of nude photographs later to a judge, and reported in the May 9th *Tribune*, "You can see that I took these pictures only for artistic purposes."

As Louise Teuber's murder investigation progressed, an impressive list of suspects emerged, including several boyfriends and ex-boyfriends, military men, known sexual deviants in the area, and Herman Newby. As noted above, a police search of the Newby home, which was only blocks from Miss Teuber's house, turned up a cache of nude photos and paintings. Under interrogation, Newby admitted to taking the photos and stated that some photographs were of the now deceased girl.

Louise Teuber was only sixteen years old when Newby first photographed her. According to testimony provided later by his wife, Newby took some photos of young women, including Louise, at the isolated Whispering Pines mountain cabin. When news of Louise posing in the nude became public, the *San Diego Union* and other papers salaciously pounced on the disclosure. *The Union* could not resist saying that, of course, photographers selected Louise as a model, "for it was said she had a rounded graceful figure." *The Union* omitted to say that her in-death nude photographs graced their coffee-stained desks. Apparently, Mr. Teuber and Louise's sister were not aware of the nude modeling assignments.

At one point, a Northern California newspaper implied that Louise was in the habit of posing nude and, while certainly not true, the innuendo again paints the victim in an unsympathetic (for the times) way. The Minneapolis' *Star Tribune* tied the modeling to her death, going so far as to state that "there is every evidence that she had disrobed willingly before death struck." As if by disrobing willingly, she brought on her tragic death.

When asked to state his whereabouts on April 18, the night of the murder, Newby said he and his wife drove to the Whispering Pines cabin to relax returning to San Diego late that night. Early newspaper accounts erroneously reported that the mountain cabin sat near to the murder scene, perhaps implicitly implicating him. Actually, Newby's cabin was located just east of the mountain town of Julian, California, over fifty miles from the murder site. Traveling on mostly two-lane roads, the trip from the cabin to San Diego would have taken more than an hour. And according to his extremely nervous wife, the couple spent the evening of the murder at the cabin and returned home late, although she did not remember how late. Given that sunset was 6:20 p.m., after nine or ten may have seemed late, especially in the 1930s. She admitted she turned in when they arrived home. She was not sure what time Herman came to bed.

Ceci Newby not only verified her husband's alibi, but she also said that she had been present the previous year when Herman took the nude photos of Louise at their cabin. Ceci had a fifteen-year-old niece, Ida May, who also chummed around with Louise at the cabin. Based entirely on Ceci's testimony, Herman Newby was apparently no longer considered a prime suspect in the murder.

Unswayed, Mr. Teuber adamantly discounted the alibi provided by Mrs. Newby. The May 9th *Tribune* reported that between sobs he said, "I believe these pictures were the cause of my daughter's death." Addressing the nude photographs, Teuber said, "We were neighbors for four years. I never thought Newby would do such a thing. I never gave him permission." Teuber told the Court that the nude photos of his young daughter were apparently "taken in January at a party at Whispering Pines on my daughter's 16th birthday." Throughout the investigation, the bereaved father continued to point the finger of accusation towards

Newby. Police disregarded the accusations as those of a bereaved father.

And after decades of research and despite the alibi provided by Ceci Newby, Herman Newby remains my number-one suspect. Even if the Newbys spent the evening at the cabin, Herman Newby could have left the house on Maryland Street in the late evening, picked Louise up, and been at the murder scene by midnight, well before the passing motorist encountered the threatening man around one thirty in the morning. But why would Ceci lie, if, in fact, she did? Let's get to that a bit later.

While the investigation into Louise's murder continued, Newby was indicted and stood trial on charges of printing and possessing indecent pictures. He took the stand in his own defense and told the judge that he was an art student and that the photos were used to create oil paintings. According to the newspapers (the court papers cannot be found), d he knew Louise had just turned sixteen when he photographed her. But she was, as he said, "mature looking and oh so beautiful." On May 9, 1931, nearly two months after Louise's murder, Herman Newby pleaded guilty to a count of possessing indecent photographs and was quickly found guilty by Superior Court Judge Arthur Munro. The judge sentenced Newby to six months in jail, which he served immediately. His name apparently never came up again as a suspect in Louise Teuber's death.

During Newby's imprisonment or shortly after his release in early November 1931, Cecile Newby filed for and was granted a divorce. The grounds were physical abuse and moral turpitude. Having served his jail time and alone for the first time in more than a decade, Herman Newby stayed in San Diego for a year. He or Ceci sold their Maryland Street house in 1932. He then moved out of San Diego to either Arkansas or Indiana, where in 1933, he married Jo Nelle Harrell, aged twenty-four years; Herman was forty-two years old. They married in her home state of Arkansas but soon moved to Indiana. Over the next few years, Herman worked at several jobs, but primarily as a steelworker.

Herman and Jo Nelle had two children together, Diane and Francis, also known as Frank. Born in 1934, Francis was an early learner and made the local newspapers when he was only three and knew all the states and their capitals. Diane was born five years later. According to Diane, her father was a mean drunk who beat both children and his wife. She told me that her father would fly into fits of rage, most often directed at women. Further, in personal letters and emails to me spanning the winter of 2017 and summer of 2018, Diane asserted he had repeatedly sexually molested her as a child and kept a cache of photographs of her in bikinis. In one of her first letters to me, she said that even though I had not accused him of murder or even implied it, Diane wrote, "My first reaction was HE DID IT."

After only six years of marriage, Jo Nelle and Herman separated in September 1939, and she soon filed for divorce. Echoing Cecile Newby's grounds for the first divorce, Jo Nelle stated in the divorce papers that she endured "cruel and inhumane treatment. The defendant is alleged to have an incorrigible temper." A year after the divorce was completed, Herman Newby was arrested and convicted on charges of assault and battery on an unnamed person near Greenfield, Indiana. Newby was fined and assessed court costs but spent no time in jail.

In the divorce, the court gave Jo Nelle custody of their one-year-old daughter Diane. Typical of custody hearings of the time, where courts often thought that boys should be raised by their father, Herman gained custody of five-year-old Francis. According to Diane Newby Powe, despite the divorce, her mother and the children intermittently stayed with Herman for twelve years afterwards. Diane believes that her mother could not stand to lose her son, who Herman said he would take far away. On one occasion in about 1941, Herman took his son on a cross-country road trip that ended in San Diego, where they stayed for a year. Jo Nelle endured until Francis was old enough to flee the household by joining the navy. Almost immediately, she left Herman for good and later remarried.

Chapter Ten

"All Women are Whores and Prick Teasers"

My first correspondence with Diane Powe, daughter of Herman Newby, took the form of a very polite, non-accusatory letter. The letter explained I was writing a history based in San Diego. I asked if her father or other family members had ever mentioned the murder of Louise Teuber or any of the murders of 1931. I pointed out that her father had lived in the same neighborhood as the murdered girl and her murder was quite sensational for the times. The letter was a long shot. Imagine my surprise and elation when Diane promptly wrote back. Over the next three years, we corresponded by regular mail and email.

Her first response came sooner than I expected. In fact, I thought the odds were 50-50 on receiving any response. Diane's welcoming letter included some chilling lines. She began by asking, "Do you know if my father was ever a suspect? My father was not a good man... he was a drunk with a violent temper. He beat my mother and my brother often and did sexual things to me when I was a very young girl. He often said that all women were whores and prick teasers. He threatened to kill us several times." Do you see some elements of a killer's profile in Herman's profane words? Yes? Me too.

Diane closed out that letter by writing, "I don't know if he ever killed anyone, but I do believe he was capable." The semi-nude condition of Louise as they found her hanging from the tree is what profiler John Douglas calls a degrading position, intending to disgrace or degrade the victim, even in death.

While Newby lay (literally) on his deathbed in a hospital, at the insistence of his family, his fifteen-year-old daughter Diane visited him one last time. Reflecting on his life, Newby told Diane that "he didn't want to die knowing that everyone hated him." She responded God loved him and when he cynically discounted that, she graciously "told him that I loved him though I didn't mean it—I don't think."

Herman Newby, age sixty-four, died on Valentine's Day 1955, and was interred in the Santa Fe, New Mexico, National Cemetery three days later. Mrs. E.R. Campbell, a family member of Herman, ordered and paid for a marble headstone from the Georgia Marble Company in Tate, Georgia. Diane did not attend the services, although her brother Frank did. With the passing of Herman Newby, any investigation into his potential role in the murder of Louise Teuber also died. But, as we shall see, perhaps that is not the case.

Why was Herman Newby apparently never a prime suspect? Based on the testimony of his wife Ceci, who said that she was with Herman at their cabin in Whispering Pines the afternoon and evening of the murder, they dropped Newby from the active suspects list. Law enforcement accepted, with far less skepticism than today, the testimony of a wife or husband or even of an upstanding person to verify an alibi. But hypothetically, why might Ceci lie for her husband in such a horrendous case? It is possible that she simply did so out of marital allegiance and/or actually believed him innocent. Or was she physically coerced into lying for her abusive husband?

However, it seems likely if Cecile did, in fact, lie that Herman forced her to lie. Keep in mind, his much-abused daughter said, "He beat my mother [Newby's second wife] and my brother often... He said that all women were whores and prick teasers. He threatened to kill us several times."

It seems possible that for his alibi in 1931, Cecile was coerced into lying to the police. Remember, one reason for the divorce was physical abuse. Perhaps she also lied about being at the Whispering Pines cabin when sixteen-year-old Louise posed for Newby. No one else came forward to verify her story. Unable to put up with his abuse and perhaps believing, or knowing, him to be a killer, Cecile left Herman, remarried, and lived out her life in peace in San Diego and finally in Julian, where she died. A longtime resident of Julian, familiar with Ceci and the Pease family told me in an interview that she could not imagine Herman being a killer or Ceci lying for him.

While we may never know for certain why Cecile might lie for her husband, if, in fact, she did; women in abusive relationships often lie for their men and cover up their violence and abuse. There is evidence that much later, Newby's second wife, Jo Nelle, also provided excuses and alibis for him in less serious run-ins with the law and that she too feared him on several levels.

The noted profiler and psychologist Dr. Deborah Schurman-Kauflin wrote an article in a 2012 *Psychology Today* regarding wives who lie for their abusers and killers: "Some play their part and aid their spouses because they fear the shame and potential judgment if the truth came out. They cannot believe such a horrible thing is happening, and if they keep it secret then somehow it is less real. In a very twisted type of thinking they would rather live with their secret and play their role in the abuse than to face shame or any potential consequences."

This could well be a description of Cecile Newby. If, however, Ceci told the truth, it is unlikely that Louise and Newby could have met up at seven o'clock when she was seen getting into an automobile downtown. Assuming, however, that the alibi was truthful, they still could have met up after nine o'clock, but that would require Louise to be with someone else for two or three hours before she could have met Newby.

With Newby in jail and the murder over six weeks old, the investigation continued. By the late 1920s and early 1930s, when Louise was murdered, criminology had strengthened by leaps and bounds in using forensics and investigation. San Diego may have been a little behind Los Angeles and San Francisco (okay, probably a lot behind), but there were good, capable local officers pursuing criminals. There were also officers who were, at best, inept. San Diego, however, like many cities across the United States, lacked state-of-the-art forensic labs and scientifically trained specialists. For those skills, cities turned to state organizations, which in California was the State Bureau of Identification out of Sacramento.

When Clarence S. Morrill was called onto the case, hope increased they would soon find the murderer. Morrill also worked for a short time on the Virginia Brooks case in March 1931. Morrill, forty-eight years of age, served as chief of the State Bureau of Identification from its inception in 1918. He was one of the first formally trained criminologists in the United States, and strongly advocated using technology and forensics to solve crimes. Morrill was well known for using fingerprinting and handwriting specialists to solve crimes.

Morrill also wanted to incorporate aircraft in the search for criminals making their escape in fast cars. He worked to develop regional road maps so that they could employ better roadblocks at key spots. A past president of the California Division of the International Association for Identification, he also favored installing teletype machines in all major California law enforcement offices. Morrill knew criminals could avoid capture and prosecution simply by moving to another city or county. Morrill strongly pushed for, and then implemented, the development of the fingerprint bank. In the decade following the murders of Virginia Brooks and Louise Teuber, most large law enforcement agencies adopted several of Morrill's techniques.

Sporting round wire-rimmed glasses and with his hair severely parted, Morrill looked every bit like a librarian or accountant. At less than one hundred forty pounds and about five feet eight inches tall, Morrill could be an intimidating figure with a stern, officious personality. Morrill arrived in San Diego on April 23rd and immediately caught the attention of the local press, where a headline proclaimed, "CRIME SPECIALIST HERE TO AID IN TEUBER INQUIRY." The newspaper then proceeded to repeatedly misspell his name as *Morrell*. Chief Morrill reviewed the existing evidence, which proved meager, and visited the crime scene. How the local investigators felt about a well-respected outsider intruding into their case is unstated. Then, as now, jealousy and turf wars amongst law enforcement agencies often clouded investigations.

Unfortunately for the Teuber murder, Morrill was soon called away to work on another case, leaving his competent assistant Harry Hickok to continue the investigation. Pressed for new information by the newspapers, on April 30th, Hickok told local reporters that regarding plausible theories and suspects, "none of them is out as of yet." Within a few days, however, Hickok too left San Diego. The case remained in the hands of befuddled local law enforcement. A newspaper account reported that in the ten days since the murder, "no arrests have been made and no motive for the crime has been established." Local authorities and the anxious populace feared that Teuber's murder would join the ranks of San Diego's unsolved murders, along with that of Virginia Brooks.

In later months, the *Los Angeles Times* and critics from Sacramento chided San Diego law enforcement for not only being unable to solve Teuber's murder but also others that occurred in 1931. *The Times* cynically wrote that maybe if investigators from Los Angeles and Sacramento had stayed on the cases, murderous fiends would be behind prison bars. Not walking Southern California streets looking for new victims. We could have saved innocent lives, they proclaimed. *The Times* labeled the overall San Diego investigation "Poor Police Work." Local law enforcement offices chaffed at the criticism but acknowledged that no progress was being made. Even the *San Diego Union* later admitted that over a six-year span, there were thirteen unsolved murders. They rhetorically asked, "When will it end, this reign of terror?"

For the Teuber case, over the next few months and even in the passing years, various investigators continued to interview suspects. Deputy Sheriff O.C. Macumber, who worked the Virginia Brooks crime scene, seemed particularly interested. Throughout the summer of 1931, he tracked down potential suspects and held several interrogations. Other investigators reanalyzed evidence and followed up on leads. The investigation dragged on.

Then, finally, a break in the case. A full banner headline in the October 1, 1931, *Tribune* dramatically and optimistically proclaimed NAB TEUBER GIRL SLAYER. According to the news account, Lowell Bell, a sixteen-year-old ex-sailor dishonorably discharged from the navy, confessed to the crime. He implicated others, including a girl to whom he wrote insipid love letters from jail. Bell said that Louise was killed in a San Diego home and hanged to make it look like a suicide. Finally, the police said, we may have our man.

Bell joined the navy at fifteen when both he and his mother lied regarding his age to get him in. They hoped to break his pattern of petty crimes. Newspapers described Bell as a not-too-smart overgrown boy with a thin, almost bony build, and an awkward gait. The *Union* on October 3rd also knowingly told its readers that Bell's eyes "lacked snap." As sports and crime writer Bill James has wryly noted, in the 1930s and continuing somewhat to this day, police officers, news writers, true crime authors, and the average person persist in seeing evil, malice, and shark-like tendencies in the eyes of malcontents. Surely "eyes that lack snap" or appear *dead* are those of a cold-blooded killer. Or not.

Local investigators brought Bell to San Diego from the Los Angeles Jail, where he was being held on several burglary charges. They took him to the oak grove murder scene to note his reaction. He seemed unmoved and nonchalant. Police stood Bell before Louise's father and sister in hopes that they might identify him. They told officers they had never seen him before. Louise's friends told police she had mentioned no one named Lowell or Bell. Besides, they said, he was much too young for her and certainly didn't look like her type.

Bell's confession looked strong, with plenty of details and even a motive. Bell told the *Union* on October 1st, that "I tried to make love to her, but she would not stand for it, and we argued." The argument turned violent, and he hit her and then hanged her. Sure, I know how to make those rope knots, he told detectives. "I'm a sailor, for God's sake." While in jail, he requested copies of the newspapers so he could read about himself. Daily, he asked if "his girl" had written him back. She had not.

Within a few days, Bell recanted his confession. The October 3rd *Union* reported that he told the police that he made up the story while in jail to impress his more hardened bunk mates. Bell also told investigators he hoped "to make the front page—I thought it would make me a big shot gangster in Chicago." One investigator concluded Bell was "just a fictionist and a publicity seeker." Another called him a freak.

Bell told the press that his entire story was based on their newspaper articles, which he read studiously. He offered his tale was "pure hokum." These kinds of confessions were and are more common than one might think. That is one reason homicide detectives often withhold certain crime scene or autopsy evidence to verify the statements of a confessor.

Bell ultimately produced an alibi for the night of April 18, saying he had been drinking with friends in south San Diego over in Shelltown at a motor hotel. In the 1930-40s, Shelltown included the area centered on 41st and Division Street on the border between South San Diego and National City. Recently, the term Shelltown has reemerged to replace a neighborhood name in the more generalized Southeast District.

When interviewed, Bell's drinking buddies verified his story. They noted Bell scooted out of San Diego shortly after their marathon drinking session. Apparently, his friend Ray Lewis had caught Bell drunk with Toodles, Lewis' wife, in their motel room. Police cleared Bell as a murder suspect and returned him to Los Angeles to stand trial on robbery and burglary charges. Assumedly, Toodles and Ray resumed their marital bliss.

Apparently unable to keep his nose clean, Bell ended up in San Quentin in April 1935, where he served a five-year term for burglary until his parole in early 1940. Which he violated and returned to San Quentin to finish his sentence in September 1940. Bell subsequently married, apparently abandoned his life of crime, had a child, and lived most of his life in Stockton, California, working as an electrician. Returning to the San Diego area late in life, Lowell Bell died in El Cajon, California, in 1995 at eighty.

In September 1933, the San Diego Police Department commissioned Deputy Sheriff Virgil P. Gray, a Los Angeles peace officer and self-described crime detector, to examine the Teuber and Brooks cases. In February 1934, he submitted his report on both cases. He audaciously declared to the press that the Louise Teuber case should be closed. Her death, he insisted, was not a homicide. With no details, and in direct opposition to the medical examiner's report,

Gray stated Teuber had likely died by suicide by hanging. According to news accounts, Sheriff Cooper then did, in fact, close the case.

For the Brooks case, Gray believed the child's killer was long gone from the San Diego area. He did, however, name the killer, although the supposed killer's name was not released and remains a mystery. Gray declared the case hopeless to pursue.

Beyond a news article or two in mid-February 1934, no other information is available for his assertions. Certainly, in later articles detailing unsolved murders in San Diego, there is no sign that police considered the Teuber case a suicide or solved or closed.

In fact, in response to a California Public Information Act request I filed in 2019, the San Diego Police Department stated that police records and investigator's notes for the Teuber case, if they have them, cannot be given to the public because the case is not officially closed. It remains an open cold case—not an "active case," as I was informed, just open.

Not content with leaving the cases unsolved, the police tried another approach. In 1935, San Diego Deputy Sheriff George Brereton, a college-trained criminal specialist, took on the unsolved cases of Louise Teuber and Virginia Brooks. Brereton reviewed the case files, pored over crime scene photographs, and conducted a series of interviews. Casting his net far afield, Brereton went to San Francisco and interviewed imprisoned murder suspect Ralph Jerome Selz, aka Slipton Fell. That's right, Slipton Fell.

Twenty-seven-year-old Selz held special interest in Brereton because of his purported use of knotted and looped ropes in his murders. In addition, there was speculation that Jerome Selz might be the mysterious and elusive "Jerry" mentioned by some of Teuber's friends. They described him as strikingly handsome in a Hollywood kind of way, charming, and always on the lookout for an attractive woman companion. He loved to joke with the police and made light of their investigations.

When arrested for another crime, Selz reportedly had a sixty-foot length of rope in the trunk of his car. Selz, known as the Laughing Murderer, teased Brereton, saying he might or might not have killed the San Diego girls. He admitted to living near Teuber's hanging site in 1931 but offered no other information. Although implicated in other murders, including that of Ada Rice, the ex-wife of the mayor of Nome, Alaska, and sentenced to life at San Quentin, Selz was apparently never a serious suspect in Teuber's murder.

But it would be perhaps unfair to Louise Teuber, the so-called happy kid, to leave her case there. Instead, let us make several assumptions and see where they take us. First, let's assume that her murderer killed her in an act of rage or passion and perhaps never killed again. Maybe it was a date gone bad. Or the killer had offered Louise a ride out of town, and they ended up near Black Mountain, where she shunned his advances.

Or she had agreed to a nude photoshoot for money to fund her trip to Chicago and something had gone terribly wrong. Regardless of the events leading up to the moment of her death, her murder would be opportunistic and not premeditated. That assumption covers a lot of ground and countless men, and myriad leads to no one person. Except to say that his homicidal actions were perhaps a singular event. This does not prevent him from being a violent or hateful person. He no doubt brought that twisted psychological package with him to Mission Gorge that night.

Why would Louise end up dead at a remote place removed from major highways or communities? It is unlikely that she would have gone there willingly with a stranger. If she went of her own volition on a date, would she nearly completely disrobe willingly outside on a fifty-five-degree night? Probably not. But if she went with a date or lover and then died of strangulation after the date turned sour and being kidnapped is not out of the question. Nor is the theory that someone killed her elsewhere and took her to the remote area where they staged a suicide. That scenario would imply that her killer or killers knew Louise had frequented the Mission Gorge party spot. Maybe he or they had been there with her. Perhaps they thought that staging a suicide there was not only out of the public's eye but also consistent with her activities.

The possibility of a photoshoot questions who the photographer might be. Besides the unknown professional photographer F.M. Jones, who told investigators he saw her get into an automobile about 7 p.m. Saturday night, only one other person comes immediately to mind. Herman Newby, who Louise had posed for nude in the past and may have trusted. If Newby, or someone else, to be fair, offered her money to pose in a natural setting for an artistic nighttime shoot, would she have done so? And would she have suggested the oak grove where she and friends had partied in the past? Possibly her killer offered the money that she so desperately sought to make her getaway from dead San Diego. Maybe suggested even a lift to the train station in Los Angeles.

It seems possible, though, that she may have posed almost nude elsewhere in a house or a cabin and some action led to her being hit and strangled. Maybe the *San Diego Union* got it right when a headline reported, "BELIEVE TEUBER GIRL SLUGGED IN SAN DIEGO ROOM." Perhaps by an enraged unwanted lover or a photographer who wanted more salacious images of her. In that scenario, Louise, still alive but perhaps unconscious, may have been wrapped in the army blanket and taken to Mission Gorge, where the suicide ruse was enacted. Lacking specific details about evidence or absence of evidence of a struggle at the hanging site, we are left with more questions unanswered than answered. Newby's daughter Diane told me in a letter that "I can see him killing her in a rage and setting the scene to draw suspicion away from him." My father was very clever, she told me. Diane asked, "Could she have been killed elsewhere?"

Next, let us revisit our earlier stated profile. The killer was a large or at least physically able white man, age somewhat indeterminate but likely between twenty-five and forty-five years old, held a low opinion of women, and given to occasional fits of rage. He probably owned an automobile, had experience tying half-hitch knots in relatively thick rope, was an organized killer, and, assuming that she had not been kidnapped, knew Louise. Maybe even held her misplaced trust.

I strongly suggest that Herman Newby, a white man, ex-navy with a knowledge of ropes and knots, alcoholic, abuser of girls and women, a highly organized individual, photographer of underage girls including Louise, wearer of a large, heavy navy ring, aged forty years, and as a man who considered all women to be "prick teasers" is a pretty good match. Regardless of whether Louise met her death at the Mission Gorge site or was killed elsewhere, Newby fits the bill. As his own daughter said, "I don't know if he ever killed anyone, but I do believe he was certainly capable."

On the other hand, Louise's aviator friend Cyril Smith also fits most of the profile He would have known about ropes and tie downs from his aviation experience, possessed an organized and precise personality, knew Louise (maybe even sexually, according to him), and was intimately familiar with the infamous oak grove. And what should we make from his statement? That he not only knew the exact tree Louise died under, but he also knew the actual cause of death—from oral sex gone wrong? Insider knowledge from his buddies, from the killer, or because he was the killer? Or was Smith just telling Thomas Jordan a boastful story from his misspent youth?

Motive. Means. Opportunity. Unindicted.

CHAPTER ELEVEN

WE FOUND A DEAD GIRL—AND RAN LIKE MAD

On a warm Sunday morning in May 1931, two young buddies were playing around the fake Indian Village buildings built for the San Diego Panama American Exposition of 1915. They modeled the village after the Zuni and Hopi pueblos of New Mexico. Zunis and Native people of Arizona and New Mexico occupied the village during the exposition. Local Indigenous people, including the Kumeyaay, were not considered romantic or exotic enough to be represented at the Exposition. The passage of time had not been kind to the temporary wire-and-stucco buildings, and even the more substantial structures needed repair. Soon there would be commissions to decide the fate of the buildings. The assumption being that most of them would be dismantled and sold for scrap. While some areas in Balboa Park were infamous as lover's lanes, the Indian Village grounds were more associated with robberies and muggings.

The Boy Scouts' headquarters occupied a portion of the abandoned village with some structural integrity, and the rest were home to pigeons and rodents. In 1927, the *San Diego Union* reported that the crumbling and barely inhabitable Boy Scouts buildings were an eyesore and an embarrassment to the city. At one point, County Coroner Schuler Kelly and other civic-minded people built a new Boy Scouts kitchen and mess hall within the dilapidated complex.

Today, the part of Balboa Park that once housed the faux Indian Village and the Boy Scouts' headquarters is, in part, a grassy patch of land that contains the War Memorial Building. In 1931, plans were afoot to build the memorial, but the actual construction was a few years off. A little to the southwest is the San Diego Zoo. Immediately to the west is an open ball field, and a little to the north and across the street is Roosevelt Middle School.

Richard Charles Roehl, aged nine, and Jess Alfred Zimmerman, aged ten, lived nearby (on Park Boulevard, and out east on Chamoune Avenue, respectively) and regularly spent their weekend days hanging out in the area. It would be a month before they finished school. They anxiously looked forward to summer vacation.

Richard sported curly blond hair, ears that projected out from his skull a little further than normal, and he usually wore a big smile. Jess had somewhat deep-set eyes, straw-colored hair, and was a little chubby. For the pals, there were canyons to explore and acres of dirt paths to run down. One well-used trail went to Mission Valley, where dairies and ranches dotted the floodplain. Kids played outdoors back then, usually unaccompanied by bothersome parents or adults. Times were different in 1931.

That Sunday morning turned out to be anything but a typical play day for the two buddies. By nearly noon, after roaming through a nearby canyon, they ended up just west of Park Boulevard. In an area covered with dying grass and dirt on the western side of the low east wall of the old Indian Village, Jess suddenly halted. He caught sight of what appeared to be a fully clothed girl.

"Oh! Golly, Dick, look what I have found!" Jess shouted.

Richard at first thought the female shape was a discarded wax mannequin but when he realized it was a real girl—a real dead girl—he joined the barefooted Jess in scurrying away as fast as they could.

As Jess told reporters, "We found a dead girl—and ran like mad," and run they did, all the way, almost a mile to Richard's house, where they breathlessly told his mother the story of their discovery. Mrs. Zimmerman, a nurse, suggested to the boys that what they saw probably was a wax figure. Careless people were always dumping rubbish over the low wall.

Jess replied, "Naw, Ma... it's a girl—and she's dead."

Mrs. Roehl immediately dialed the police and then walked the boys back to the discovery site. Deputy Coroner David Gershon took the call at 12:50 p.m. and alerted police.

"My God!" Mrs. Roehl exclaimed. "The kids are right; there is a dead girl lying amongst fallen wooden posts and trash."

The ensuing newspaper coverage, investigation, and trial would push the hanging of Louise Teuber from the headlines and then from the news altogether. Louise became old news even as her murder investigation wore on. The news axiom that *if it bleeds, it leads* rose in full force, and Hazel had bled—a lot.

Hazel Bradshaw, a twenty-two-year-old brunette with curly hair and blue eyes, stood five feet two inches and weighed about one hundred thirty pounds. Several newspaper accounts including those in the *Union*, *Tribune*, and *Sacramento Bee*, describe Hazel as "exceptionally beautiful," "stunning," and "pretty." Hazel worked as a clerk and telephone operator at the Downtown San Diego office of the Santa Fe Railway Company at 300 Broadway. Together, she and her sister Mildred, who was also a clerk and a waitress at a drive-in sandwich shop, supported the family, which included nine children.

Her father, Charles, who was seventy-one in 1931, was slowly going blind. He worked as a lumberman and a laborer, but the work was only occasional. Her mother, Cora, aged fifty-one, was a homemaker. To supplement their income, she occasionally took in laundry and dry cleaning. A small terrier mix kept the family company. Hazel's neighborhood surrounding her house at 4510 Alabama Street was solidly middle class, perhaps only a little less so than Louise Teuber's area. Her neighbors hailed from California, the Midwest, England, France, and Mexico. Many, but not the majority, had a radio set, including the Bradshaw family. Most were renters who paid between thirty and forty dollars a month for a typical twelve hundred square foot two-bedroom cottage or bungalow.

At thirty dollars a month, the Bradshaws were paying a little more than the average San Diego rent (twenty dollars a month), but they were living in a well-kept, relatively new neighborhood. Many of her older neighbors owned autos, although the majority walked the six blocks up to Park Boulevard to catch the Number 7 streetcar. Streetcar Number 7 ran up and down Park Boulevard from Broadway on the south, and past University Avenue and El Cajon Boulevard on the north. Occupations of her neighbors included attorney, theater manager, salesman, laborer, nurse, mechanic, and barber. Most had attended some level of school, with many graduating high school.

Hazel dated a fair amount, including older men, and especially enjoyed going to movies. One of her steady dates, Moss E. Garrison, worked with Hazel. He lived downtown and frequently met her after work for dinner or to take in a movie. They had their choice of over ten movie houses in the downtown core. If the weather was good, they often walked back to her house on Alabama Street to save the twenty-five-cent streetcar fare. On the last evening of her life, Hazel and Moss took in two movies. They then walked north up Fifth Avenue, then east across the beautifully arched Laurel Street Bridge, and turned north towards her home. Today, I can't imagine most young men and women walking over four miles from a movie theater to home. Or two miles or even a mile. As with so many things in these stories, it was a different time.

With police alerted to the dead body in Balboa Park, a full-scale investigation began. Detective Fred "Jerry" Lightner and motorcycle Officer Harry Travis handled the initial stage of the in-field investigation. Chief of Police Arthur Hill, who had worked on the Virginia Brooks case, and Captain of Detectives Paul J. Hayes, who also worked on the Brooks murder, arrived soon after. The crime scene was relatively secluded, especially in the evening hours, although this part of the park had a reputation as a sometimes lover's lane and a place to sip a little wine. A low faux-adobe wall would have obscured the body from any casual passersby walking on the adjacent path. The buildings of the pueblo blocked any view from the east side near Park Boulevard. The investigators took crime scene photos, searched in vain for the murder weapon, and took notes on the disposition of the body and blood splatter. A morgue truck arrived and took Hazel to the Bonham Brothers Mortuary for the autopsy.

Hazel's personal effects included a white Waltham wristwatch that had stopped at 9:43, although whether that was in the evening or morning was uncertain. She also wore white beads strung with yellow metal, and carried a tan purse containing a compact, a portion of a candy bar, and seventy-eight cents. Recently worried about her weight, she had slipped a penny into an ornate scale near a movie theater and gotten not only her weight (*a little too high*, she thought, according to later court testimony) but also a fortune. A slip of paper from the combination scale and fortune-telling machine mistakenly assured Hazel that "Your path should be a comparatively smooth one, with no great gain and no great loss. You will, therefore, go on rising and improve your position by sticking to it." The ambiguity of her paper fortune was far surpassed by the certainty of her death.

She wore a print dress and a light silk coat. Underneath her dress, Hazel wore a light and airy Step In, a thin chemise often made of silk or thin cotton popular at the time with the younger set, those Modern Girls. Her hard, low-heeled pumps were snuggly strapped to her feet. Her hat lay crumpled under her lifeless head.

Being a Sunday, Dr. Elliott G. Colby, who maintained a private practice and served as an on-call autopsy surgeon, notified Deputy Coroner Gershon. Gershon performed the autopsy less than an hour after the body arrived at the mortuary. Dr. Colby, aged thirty-four years, had recently moved to San Diego from Yuma, Arizona, and set up practice in the Bank of Italy (now Bank of America) Building. He had taken a role in the earlier autopsy of little Virginia Brooks, assisting Dr. Toomey. Dr. Colby would be in charge of the documentation of Gershon's findings. After the inquest, the *San Diego Evening Tribune* on May 11th quoted Colby. He said there was a deep knife thrust slightly above Hazel's right breast, which severed the pulmonary artery, causing almost immediate death.

Colby also noted several other knife wounds. Dr. Colby wrote Hazel suffered a knife wound one-and-a-half inches in length on the top of her left shoulder that extended into her shoulder joint. He recorded another severe wound measuring two inches downward from her clavicle and into her lung. A much larger, ragged wound that measured three-and-a-half inches cut across her left clavicle. Colby told the press that Hazel valiantly struggled and fought with her attacker. Both hands showed deep lacerations on her fingers, thumb, and palms from her attacker yanking the knife back. Dr. Colby surmised Hazel incurred upper body wounds while upright and desperately fighting for her life. The six wounds below her breasts were more like puncture wounds inflicted after she had fallen.

Some darkened depressions on her neck were not from strangulation but from the chain of beads she wore. Initially,

Colby estimated the time of death at ten to twelve hours before the discovery of the body, given what he described as the moderate stage of rigor mortis. That would place her death at between midnight and 2:30 a.m. The May 11, 1931, death certificate signed by Dr. Elliott G. Colby, for Hazel, lists the cause of death as "stab wounds of left chest with lacerations of left lung and left pulmonary artery by party or parties unknown."

As shown in the autopsy sketch, the major wounds were on Hazel's left side, with eleven wounds illustrated. Stabs on the front left side of a person typically show the killer held the knife in their right hand. Colby also stated that based on the wounds, the knife was a large double-sided style. More like a hunting or butcher knife than a smaller folding knife. Later at trial, Colby testified that the smaller wounds were inflicted first, including defensive wounds on her hands, and that the large, deep wound above her right breast was the one that killed her. Hazel also suffered some sort of blunt force to her chin that left a one-inch bruise.

The official report noted that the large double-edged blade first passed through Hazel's dress and then her underslip. As shown in the autopsy sketch, estimates put the width of the blade at one and a half inches. That some of the deeper knife wounds were wider than an inch and a half showed that the blade cut fresh flesh, as much as three and a half inches, as it tore through the body.

The autopsy revealed no evidence of vaginal bruising, and they found no sperm on or in the body. The coroner reported Hazel was not pregnant and had not been assaulted. *Assault* being the polite contemporary code word for raped or sexually molested. Her stomach contained a small clot of blood but no sign of food, showing it had been several hours between her last food intake and her death. The absence of undigested food in her stomach would be a key point in the later murder trial.

The rear of her Step In bore a slight brownish discoloration from fecal matter and smudges of dirt and grass stains. The dirt and grass stains substantiated the autopsy report that at some point Hazel had lain in a prone position on her back. Close to two paces from her body, a large pool of dry, darkening blood stained the brown soil. Whether pooled blood showed Hazel met her death at the site or elsewhere was never satisfactorily determined. While left unsaid, the apparent lack of blood splatter probably showed the initial attack took place somewhere else.

The time of death through determination of postmortem rigidity, or rigor mortis, is of course, commonly used but poorly understood outside of the medical profession. Variables such as physical exertion of the deceased prior to death can speed up the depletion of oxygen in the body and thus speed up rigor mortis. Overweight people enter rigor mortis at a slower rate, and, importantly, with Hazel Bradshaw, the air temperature affected the rate of rigor mortis.

In Hazel's case, establishing an accurate time of death proved somewhat inconclusive given that the evening and morning of the third was warm and the body had been in at least partial sun for part of the late morning. Her efforts to resist the killer would have been a major exertion and depletion of oxygen. At the trial, the ambiguous time of death became a crucial factor in determining guilt or innocence.

Considering the overall stiffness of her body, the coroner initially estimated death somewhere between twelve hours and possibly twenty-four hours before discovery. Around noon the day before, which was not possible, or on the conservative side near midnight the night before—quite a spread. At the trial, after more than an hour of questioning by defense attorney Fairchild, Deputy Coroner Elliot G. Colby changed his estimate, stating that death had occurred shortly before midnight or a few hours after midnight.

This contradicted his earlier statement that death occurred sometime between 9 p.m. Saturday evening and 9 a.m. Sunday morning. He gave no reason for reducing the timeline, but Colby apparently went with a shorter period, reflecting the air temperature, Hazel's body mass, and her possible physical exertion. As we will see, the defense's expert witness, ex-coroner Kelly Schuyler, postulated a far different time of death. Reasonable doubt.

On her death certificate, completed on May 11th, they gave the cause of death as lacerations and stab wounds inflicted by "party or parties unknown. Homicide." Elliot Colby, MD, autopsy surgeon, and Chester D. Gunn, coroner, signed the certificate. At trial, Dr. Colby would be intensely grilled about his findings and what appeared to be contradictions.

After the removal of Hazel's body, they roped the crime scene off and repeatedly searched for evidence. The search focused on determining if Miss Bradshaw had been killed on-site or dumped there from another murderous location. Initially, local newspapers fostered the idea that she might have died at a "Murder House" or "Killer's Lair." Investigators determined that the killer and Hazel, while still alive, may have squeezed through a small hole in a fence to enter the inner walled area. Or that she had been dragged through the hole while drugged or already dead.

If the killer used chloroform to knock Hazel out, it would not have been in her blood and thus not revealed in the autopsy. Yet the area on either side of the entry hole apparently did not show signs of a scuffle or drag marks in the soft soil. It appeared to some investigators to be more likely that she and her murderer crawled through the hole and that she was stabbed nearby. Yet the relative sparseness of blood at the scene seemed to show otherwise.

As is always the case, they emphasized finding the murder weapon, which was assumed to be a relatively large knife. Yet in the two days immediately following her death and the discovery of her body, the crime scene apparently remained accessible to the public. Two days after the murder, on May 5th, a local boy playing around the crime scene discovered a knife on a ledge, jutting from the fake boulders a few feet from where Hazel had lain dead.

As news reporters stood around breathlessly awaiting a storyline before deadlines, police rushed the knife to police headquarters for analysis. The knife, however, proved to be far too narrow and short to have been the murder weapon. More likely, some Boy Scout lost the knife at one of the campouts. Perhaps spurred on by the false lead and public pressure, police and firefighters then burned off dry grass that matted the area. A better view of the crime scene produced no new results. A controlled burn, of course, also destroyed any other perishable evidence that may have existed within the crime scene. They did not find the murder knife there or anywhere else. The lack of the murder weapon seriously affected the trial.

Newspapers constantly reminded their readers that the Bradshaw murder was the third such death in recent months. Some suggested a single mass killer might be on the loose. The publicity and clamor from the public forced police and investigators to take fast action. The apparent inability of the San Diego Police Department and sheriff's office to solve murders came to the attention of the Los Angeles press. Social critic and sometimes humorist Harry Carr offered his reflections in his May 6th *The Lancer* column that appeared in the *Los Angeles Times*.

Carr wrote under the heading A DETECTIVE TRIUMPH:

> The talented detective force of San Diego has triumphantly solved another murder mystery. The captain of detectives boldly states that Hazel Bradshaw was stabbed to death either by her lover, Garrison, or by another lover or by some unknown person who kidnapped her. He has not,

as yet, announced his probable final conclusion that she kidnapped herself, stabbed herself to death and then threw her own body over the adobe wall. San Diego is certainly the place where they raise Philo Vances.

Philo Vances was the fictional hero sleuth of several popular detective stories of the time. Vances was a snobby dilettante who used cold, hard reasoning to solve even the most mysterious murders. Beginning in 1930, a series of six movies, including one with William Powell, brought Vances to the silver screen. Carr's piece practically dripped with acidic satire. Unlike the San Diego police, Vances always got his man. Editorials in local and state-wide newspapers also criticized the police and sheriff's departments. One *Union* editorial asked, "A Brooks case, a Teuber case, a Bradshaw case—what will be the next name in the series?" Many San Diegans wondered the same thing.

CHAPTER TWELVE

HEARTBROKEN SUITOR OR ENRAGED KILLER?

As is often the case, police investigators focused their attention on who they considered to be the most likely suspect. Moss Garrison, Louise's date the night of her death, fit the bill. Apparently, police did not actively search for other suspects. Later, the public would soundly criticize their narrow focus. In their defense, Garrison fit several criteria. He was the last person to see Hazel. He worked in a commissary, so he apparently knew his way around knives. He might, or might not, have been jilted by Hazel, and, at least to some pundits and reporters, he led a mysterious life. His landlady suggested he was rarely home and did not avail himself to either the boarding house laundry service or its communal baths. Investigators looked in vain for his supposed hidden lair, which they and the newspapers dubbed the "Murder House" or "Fiend's Lair."

Reading of Hazel's murder in the afternoon papers, and knowing he would be a suspect, Garrison turned himself in to the San Diego police on the early evening of May 3rd. At a later preliminary hearing, William E. Warner, who later joined the police force, testified Garrison played cards at a downtown cardroom on Third Street all afternoon. When they both read the news accounts of Hazel's murder, Garrison later told the Court he exclaimed, "I think that is my girlfriend!" Warner told him he better go to the police station pronto.

When the press found out Garrison had become the number-one suspect, they focused their journalist floodlights on him. Florid and sometimes lurid descriptions filled the local newspapers throughout early June and into July. Garrison became the "middle aged suitor" and "divorced man" early in the investigation, perhaps implying something untoward in dating a younger woman. The local press also found the phrases "suspected knife wielder," and "alleged little man with a big knife" to be good descriptors.

Moss Garrison stood about five feet six inches, slightly built, with blue eyes and thinning brown hair. His speech belied a pronounced Southern drawl. Garrison seemed to always be, as an acquaintance described him at trial, "bouncy." The *Union* labeled him as the "jaunty little southerner." Before moving to San Diego, Moss was a long-time resident of Atlanta, Georgia, where he owned and operated a downtown drugstore. As a youth, he was involved in an altercation where he was accused of stealing from his employer. In a small room, surrounded by three men and fearing for his life, he told Atlanta police he pulled a pistol and fired off a shot. A bullet struck the store's owner, J.P. Allen, inflicting a non-life-threatening wound. Found guilty of assault, Garrison served three months in jail and one year on a chain gang.

Shortly after his release, he married at nineteen, had a daughter who died at nine years old, and then divorced before he came to California. He worked in the commissary at the same railroad office as Hazel. Coworkers and management described him as a good worker and affable. Hazel had met Moss at a backcountry company picnic in Jacumba the previous year and they had dated on and off over that time. Garrison maintained that at one point the previous year, he and Hazel were engaged, but by mutual agreement, they broke it off.

Captain Paul J. Hayes, who would retire mid-investigation on June 15th, led the homicide investigation.

With over twenty years on the force, and fifty years of age, Hayes had a reputation as brash and short with others. His peers described him as hard-nosed and a no-nonsense kind of guy. He defended harsh interrogation methods. Some reports said he carried a blackjack to hasten arrests. As head of the homicide division, Fred E. "Jerry" Lightner, an ex-navy man, took over the case but continued to rely on Captain Hayes to assist him in bringing Garrison to trial. From the start, both men were stubbornly convinced that Garrison was the murderer.

Abijah Fairchild, a well-respected local lawyer and ex-district attorney, served as Garrison's defense attorney. Fairchild brought in Moss's brother Carson Garrison, also referred to as A.C., and Monte Clark, a private investigator from Los Angeles, to help in his defense. Carson had served in the infantry in France in World War I and was known for his dogged determination and fierce loyalty to his brother. Monte Clark, like many private investigators of the time, was self-proclaimed in his profession, although he possessed some sleuthing and research skills. In the 1930s and 1940s, it was not uncommon for both police investigators and the accused to use private investigators to ferret out otherwise unobtainable sources and facts. Often private investigators had more connections than the police and, when sufficiently paid, ample time to pursue leads.

Police interrogation in the years before and after Garrison's arrest could be brutal at worst and marginally unsavory. On more than one occasion, innocent men sued the San Diego Police Department for false arrests and brutal interrogation techniques. Garrison and his attorney would maintain before and after his trial that the police used physical force and coercion to intimidate him.

As reported in the July 25th *Union*, Garrison later said in court that on the day he turned himself in to the police for questioning, "One of the officers to whom I surrendered at the police station on May 3rd immediately said, 'You murdered Hazel Bradshaw, didn't you?' And I replied, 'I most certainly did not. I loved her and took her safely home last night.'" Garrison steadfastly held to his story of walking Hazel to her home and departing around midnight. Police locked him behind a solid steel door in cell thirteen. The next morning, he was given a "cup of cold coffee grounds and a dry slice of bread." Moss ate the bread but "couldn't go the coffee."

Not persuaded, and in a scene straight out of a black-and-white film noir, Garrisson told the Court that Acting Police Chief James Patrick then pulled his snub-nosed pistol from his leather shoulder holster and shouted at Garrison that he would "blow your brains out if you don't come clean." Another time, Garrison heard terrible screams coming from a female inmate in a nearby cell. He then overheard two detectives talking as they took a smoke break. One said to the other, "That ought to scare him and remind him of Hazel's screams. He will certainly confess everything in the morning."

Frightened but unmoved, Garrison continued to proclaim his undying love for Hazel and his innocence. According to the newspapers, one police officer tried the ruse of declaring that Hazel was unfaithful and "going around with at least a dozen other men." I'd be plenty jealous too, the cop said, just plead guilty and I will see that you won't get the maximum, the death penalty. Of course, no police officer could make such a guarantee. But lying to suspects then, as now, sometimes produced results.

At trial, Captain Hayes told the jurors that in trying to get a rise out of Garrison, he rousted him from sleep and asked if he dreamed of the murdered girl. Garrison resolutely told him no. Hayes pressed on, asking why he would not dream of his curly-haired, blue-eyed girlfriend with the winning smile. Garrison showed no sign of emotion and said again he didn't dream of her.

Despite such intimidation, ten lengthy interrogations, and after weeks in jail without the benefit of posting bond, Garrison steadfastly maintained his innocence. Avery McCue, an ex-navy man and neighbor of the Bradshaws, came forward and told Captain Hayes that he had been near the Bradshaw house the night of the murder. As he smoked a couple of cigarettes while waiting to get into a locked home sometime between 12:30 and 1 in the morning, he had seen a young woman who looked to be Hazel pacing the deserted street. Finally, a dark automobile, possibly a 1927 Studebaker, slowed to a stop and when it pulled away, the young woman was not there. Initially, Hayes said if McCue's story held up, he would have to "tear down the whole case we have built up against Garrison."

Surprisingly, after a brief interview with McCue, Hayes told the press he attached little importance to his story and "cast McCue's story into the discard." Perhaps for that reason, McCue was not slated to be called as a witness at the formal inquest, although Captain Hayes had said earlier that McCue would be a witness and he had even subpoenaed him.

Threats against Garrison came not only from the police within the confines of a dank interrogation room. While in jail, Garrison received at least two threatening letters. The full contents of one were not disclosed but implied that if the police did not do their duty, angry members of the public would. A portion of the letter repeated in the local newspapers read, "The best place for you is in jail. The public may need to take matters into its own hands." A letter from an "A.M. Henry" quoted in the May 9th *Tribune* and *Sacramento* Bee and the May 10th *Union* said, in part, "Poor little Hazel never got home Saturday night. If the police are unable to secure sufficient evidence to hold you, I will come forth with what I know." Police heard nothing from the elusive Mr. Henry or what he supposedly knew over the course of the investigation or trial.

While some elements of the population held police departments in low esteem and thought that other forms of frontier justice, like beatings or even lynchings, should prevail, such threats had to be taken seriously. Only two years later, a mob of citizens in San Jose, California, stormed the jail and dragged two confessed killers of department-store heir Brooke Hart into the town plaza. Then, while the event was being broadcast live by radio and flashbulbs lit up the night air, both men were hanged. Despite pleas from the local police, California Governor James "Sunny Jim" Rolph, uttering what might today be called a dog whistle, implied that he supported vigilante justice. Governor Rolph refused to call out the national guard before the lynchings.

On May 11th, the day of the formal inquest, the futile search for little Virginia Brooks' killer continued, the city council voted to build a dam in Mission Gorge (they did not construct it), and rioters in Spain burned several pro-government churches. Newly appointed Chief of Police Percy Benbough, a political insider with no law enforcement background, proclaimed he would do everything in his power to apprehend what he called San Diego's "mass murderer." Moss Garrison sat in jail for the eighth day.

Deputy Coroner Dave Gershon officiated the inquest. The inquest jury comprised nine men and one woman, including A. Kilerease, a businessperson, and Mrs. E.O. Gottwalls from National City. Held at Bonham Brothers mortuary at 10 a.m., the chapel, balcony, hallways, and sidewalk in front of Elm and Fourth Streets teemed with gawkers well before that time. Mrs. Bradshaw wore a plain black dress, and an old-styled black hat. She occasionally sobbed into her lace handkerchief during the inquest.

Captain Hayes had ordered that Garrison appear at the inquest unshaven and dressed in the clothes he had worn when he turned himself in the week before. Hayes told reporters he hoped that in doing so, some witnesses might have their memory jogged. Fairchild complained they should not force his client to show up looking "like a tramp and a degenerate." As a result, Garrison could shave but appeared in his wrinkled blue serge suit.

Physical evidence presented at the inquest included the autopsy report; police reports from the scene; investigators' notes; Hazel's ripped and bloodstained clothing; and the clothes worn by Garrison. The murder weapon was conspicuous by its absence. There were no eyewitnesses to the murder in spite of pleas to the public. Mrs. Bradshaw kept her composure until her daughter's clothing was held out less than ten feet from her. She then broke down and sobbed. An ex-suitor of Hazel's, Ulysses S. Wilson, on leave from ship duty so he could testify, attempted to console her.

The inquest board emphasized what appeared to be bloodstains on the edges of Garrison's pants pockets. Captain Hayes pointed out the presence of wild oat spears from Garrison's pants cuffs. Asked about what he saw at the crime scene, Richard Roehl suggested Hazel had been gagged. Hayes was quick to correct the young man, saying that it was just facial discoloration.

Avery McCue attended the inquest, despite not being called as a witness by Captain Hayes. An intrepid newspaper reporter who thought McCue's story should be heard drove McCue. McCue told the jury that he had seen Hazel get into an automobile near Polk and Alabama Streets near to her home. McCue noted the time was after midnight and closer to 1 a.m., well after Garrison said he walked her home. Garrison's attorney Fairchild called McCue's statement "the most important bit of evidence unearthed so far to prove the innocence of the man now suspected of the crime." Another neighbor, Mrs. Lyda Pfanstiel, corroborated McCue's statement but was less certain about the identity of the young woman she saw around the same time on the street.

Almost immediately after his testimony, McCue received death threats from an anonymous person in Pasadena.

In a bizarre twist, and for some inexplicable reason, the person making the threats signed the threatening letter with symbols used by the Ku Klux Klan. In this case, the symbol was a squared-off cross with a drop of blood in the center. The symbols may have just been a bit of added drama and ominous warning. The local branch of the KKK, with offices at 30th Street and University Avenue in North Park, hurriedly disavowed any connection to any aspect of the murder or the letter writer. As reproduced in the local press, the half-printed, half-cursive letter read:

> You big liar. You did not see Hazel Bradshaw. If you say you did, and Garrison is freed, Garrison and his brother will be burned and we will get Fairchild also. We'll hang you up to a tree upside down and riddle you with bullets.

Then, as now, crank letters and telephone calls in high-profile cases were to be expected. The detectives proclaimed the letter as a phony and moved on with the case. They offered no police protection to McCue or Fairchild. Garrison, of course, remained safe in jail.

On the advice of his attorney, Garrison refused to testify at the coroner's inquest, saying, "I am willing to answer any questions they wish to ask me in court." Some members of the public, reporters, and certainly the police took that statement as a guilty stance. After all, some people asked, if he was so innocent, why not tell the inquest panel what he knew? Despite the long-standing rule limiting self-incrimination, jurors and the populace look askance at suspects who invoke it. At the inquest, Garrison seemed only mildly interested in the testimony and the photographs of the crime scene. Newspaper accounted described him as stoic, even detached.

In their concluding remarks, the inquest jury pointed a crooked finger of suspicion at Garrison but said only that "[t]he evidence strongly points to one Moss E. Garrison."

In an interview after the inquest, Mr. Kilerease remarked, "We could see bloodstains on the pocket areas of Garrison's trousers." Hayes' ploy of having Garrison appear without a change of clothes had apparently worked. At the same interview, Mrs. Gottwalls said the verdict was an easy one. Garrison had brutally murdered his girlfriend. Both the jury and defense attorney Fairchild thanked Deputy Coroner Dave Gershon for conducting such a professional and well-organized inquest.

That day, District Attorney Whelan issued a formal warrant for Moss Garrison's arrest. In issuing the warrant, Whelan told the press that he "wished he had a stronger case but there was enough evidence to issue the warrant." Judge Eugene Daney signed off on the warrant for Garrison's arrest and continued incarceration without bail. Serving the warrant in his jail cell, they formally arrested Garrison the following day. The complaint noted that Garrison" "[t]hen and there willfully, unlawfully, feloniously and of his malice aforethought, did kill and murder one Hazel Bradshaw, a human being."

While the Hazel Bradshaw investigation wore on, they held her funeral services on May 12th at Merkley Mortuary on Fifth Avenue, a place that Moss and Hazel would have walked past around 11 p. m. on that fateful Saturday night only eight days before. A lot had changed over those eight days. Hazel was dead, and they jailed Moss as the primary, perhaps only, suspect. Ironically, two weeks before Hazel Bradshaw's services, teenaged Louise Teuber had laid in state in the same cold room.

Hundreds of people, including Bradshaw family members, attended the funeral services. Captain Hayes had denied Moss Garrison's request to attend the services. As the rites got under way, Reverend Williams, the minister in charge, admonished some members of the assembly, accusing them of being gawkers and morbid curiosity seekers. His flowing white robe seeming to shake as he told them they should all be there only to say farewell to the unfortunate girl and to honor God. They should come in piety, not seeking entertainment.

Banked with flowers, the casket was open for viewing. Attendees remarked that the mortuary staff did a great job of making Hazel look beautiful and serene. Cora Bradshaw slowly walked to the casket and placed a single carnation on the breast of her slain daughter. This was the second time in less than a year that Mrs. Bradshaw had buried one of her children. An adult son had been shot and killed in a fight that he was not involved in while stationed in Pensacola, Florida. Charles Bradshaw Jr. allegedly got between two men fighting over a woman in a roadhouse brawl and killed. Charles' body returned to San Diego for burial. His widow lived in San Diego at the time of his murder.

Hazel's sister Bobbie gently folded back the fine netting covering Hazel's face and placed a last kiss on her rouged cheek. Stepping away with uncertainty, Bobbie was near collapse and had to be helped in her seat. A news reporter for the May 12th *Tribune* wrote the casket was situated in such a way that "the face of the slain girl, pallid in death and drawn, but yet still beautiful, was in view of the mourners." Hazel was buried at Greenwood Park with family, friends, and hordes of onlookers still in attendance.

Twenty days later, on June 2, 1931, saw the principal players in the Bradshaw murder case at a preliminary hearing before Superior Court Judge Daney. After almost a month in jail, defense attorney Abijah Fairchild sought, at a minimum, to have his client released from jail on bail. Or in the best-case scenario, the case tossed out altogether. San Diego Deputy District Attorney Bristow worked closely with Captain Hayes to ensure that Garrison stayed in jail and that the case proceeded to trial.

It was not unusual at the time to have police officers and detectives play a major role in influencing prosecutors and district attorneys. Captain Hayes, however, seemed to maintain a particular interest in this case, perhaps because of the department's ongoing failures to solve the Brooks and Teuber cases. Here, he may have thought, was at last a viable suspect and a chance for conviction. Besides, he was about to retire and wanted to go out on a high note. Hayes seems to have made a point of trying the case in the court of public opinion by new releases and interviews.

During the preliminary hearing, heated exchanges between attorneys Fairchild and Bristow drew loud applause and cheers from the overflowing crowd in Judge Daney's small courtroom. The public often considered murder trials and hearings as a spectator sport. After all, the price of admission was free. At one point, the agitated judge ordered bailiffs to clear the courtroom so that the hearing could proceed. When things settled down, Deputy District Attorney Bristow said that Garrison's failure to contact the Bradshaw family or to view the slain woman's body was a tacit admission of his guilt. Garrison retorted he went to the police first because Warner counseled him to do so. Also, he said, because it was the right thing to do. Further, he had hoped that they would then show him the body, which they ultimately did.

At another stage of a preliminary hearing, Garrison's trousers were introduced as evidence. From the witness box, Captain Hayes told the Court that oat spears in the pants cuffs were identical to those growing at the murder scene. Fairchild, at one point, held them up to better inspect them. When he dismissively tossed them back on the defense table, Garrison casually got up from his chair and looked into the cuffs. Hayes literally leapt from the witness box and ripped the pants from Garrison. Ultimately, after ten days of proceedings, Judge Daney again denied bail for Garrison and ordered him to stand trial on the charge of murder.

The trial of Moss Garrison for the murder of Hazel Bradshaw opened on a sweltering day on July 20, 1931, in the stuffy second-floor courtroom of Judge Lawrence N. Turrentine a little over two and a half months after Hazel's murder. Judge Daney had been reassigned to other cases to reduce the growing backlog of criminal trials. In the 1930s, the concept of a speedy trial was more than a platitude. Most court systems firmly believed that sufficient evidence could be gathered and cases for the defense and prosecution made in less than three months. In some ways, Judge Turrentine, aged thirty-nine years, seemed an odd choice to preside over a sensationalized murder trial. He had only been on the superior court bench for a little over a year. A graduate of the University of California School of Law, most of his prior cases had been civil suits with only a few felonies and homicides.

As the preliminaries for the trial began, newspapers reported Garrison "wore a light-weight gray suit that was neatly pressed." His whole appearance seemed "jaunty" as he greeted various acquaintances and supporters. The jury boiled down to nine men and three women. In California, women achieved the right to serve as jurors in 1917, although some local jurisdictions, especially in rural areas, frequently seated all-male juries. The prosecution exempted three prospective jurors, using two of their challenges to eliminate women. When Judge Turrentine inquired why the women were challenged, prosecutors said it was, of course, not because they were women. But no other reason was given. Turrentine did not press the issue.

Five prospective jurors were released because of their opposition to the death penalty when a case was based on circumstantial evidence. Then, as now, implementing the death penalty elicited varying responses from the populace. Earlier, in the Virginia Brooks case, the editorial pages brimmed with suggestions for how the murderer, when apprehended, should be executed.

To make executions less barbaric, some states were experimenting with the electric chair. From the first execution by electric current in 1890, several states increasingly embraced Old Sparky. But not California. The California legislature and courts deemed death by electrocution cruel and unusual punishment, opting instead to humanely hang those convicted of capital offenses. Death by injection was over thirty-five years in the future.

One of the excused jurors opposed to the death penalty was H.L. Benbough, a well-known local furniture merchant, bon vivant, and the brother of Percy Benbough, the recently appointed (but soon-to-resign) chief of police. When the prosecution asked a prospective juror if he followed the murder story in the newspapers, the man responded that he did not believe everything he read in the papers. The gallery spectators chuckled. Another man admitted that he had to the inquest but only because his wife was curious and made him.

The twelve seated jurors comprised a cross section of middle and upper-middle class white San Diego residents. The majority were Republicans in a predominately Republican town, although Clyde Kelly, an engineer at a fish cannery, was a self-proclaimed socialist. At least four jurors owned their own homes, with the most expensive being fifteen thousand dollars and the least expensive five thousand dollars. By comparison, the average home in Depression-era San Diego sold for close to four thousand dollars.

The three female jurists were all listed as homemakers, and the known occupations of the men included a "capitalist." That juror, J. Russell Jones, owned a fifteen-thousand-dollar home on Elliott Street in Loma Portal, which in today's real estate market would fetch close to two million dollars. Other occupations included an automobile dealer, sales agent, radio repairman, electric lineman, and a real estate broker. Fellow jurists elected the capitalist J. Russell Jones to be the jury foreman. Once seated, Judge Turrentine cautioned the jurors that the trial might go on for up to ten days. He warned the prosecution and defense that if the trial wore on, he would hold night court. Hoping to speed up the trial, the judge even held the proceedings into the early evenings rather than adjourning at the more standard 3:30 or 4:30.

Abijah Fairchild, Moss Garrison's attorney, was a large man with thick hands. He had carefully groomed hair except for the bald spot that dominated the center of his head, and a wise-appearing face with slight jowls. His dark brown eyes sometimes held a mischievous glint to them. In court, he liked to introduce a little levity to the proceedings. From his office in the First National Bank Building at Ninth and Broadway, it was only a short walk to the courthouse. Along the way, he could get a shoeshine for a dime and a good Cuban cigar for a nickel.

In his early twenties, Fairchild was Corporal Fairchild in the Marine 9th Infantry. After military service, he married Lulu, the love of his young life. By the time of the Garrison trial, they had been married twenty years and were well-established on the San Diego social scene. At fifty-five, Fairchild had quite the resumé, including a successful private practice in Union, Oregon, and then serving as a district attorney in Enterprise Wallows in Oregon.

Fairchild passionately told the press that, "In all my years as an attorney, never was I more convinced of a man's innocence." Moss's brother, Carson, assisted Fairchild, and for reasons never made clear, a county social worker Mrs. Jean Haddock helped the defense.

The prosecution, led by Deputy District Attorney Samuel A. Bristow and assisted by Oran N. Muir, clearly disagreed and cited substantial evidence collected by Captain Paul Hayes. Fifty-five-year-old Bristow stood average for the time and might be described as paunchy, with a ruddy complexion, and a spoke with a Midwestern accent. Muir, fifty-six years of age, was a tall man, with a build that had once been slender but was showing signs of the good life, aged scotch, and restaurant meals at the U.S. Grant Hotel. His gray eyes matched his thinning gray hair. Bristow, who could be contentious in the courtroom, some said petty, agreed that the evidence was circumstantial, as some had labeled it. But, he said, it was also substantial and damning. In his eyes, the lack of witnesses to the murder, coupled with no murder weapon, was no roadblock. They had convicted plenty of murderers on strong circumstantial evidence.

Garrison's trial was well-attended and relatively sedate when compared to the earlier preliminary hearings, which became a media sensation with unruly crowds that overflowed the courtroom and halls. Ultimately, a lottery system controlled access and even then, spectators lined up with their brown paper lunch sacks and black Thermos bottles of coffee hours before the trial began. The local and Los Angeles press vied for seats and for positions where the photographers could capture the most emotive pictures. Members of the Bradshaw family—including Charles, Cora, and Bobbie—sat in the front-row gallery benches. Charles sported a bushy moustache and wore thick spectacles behind which his eyes sometimes closed for long periods of time. Cora and her daughter wore lace-trimmed dresses and repeatedly dabbed their eyes with linen handkerchiefs. When Hazel's blood-splattered and torn clothing was shown, Cora quickly turned away, sobbing.

The prosecution insistently maintained that Hazel had never made it home to the Bradshaw house, as Garrison said. Instead, they pounded on the idea that Garrison and Hazel had stopped near the Indian Village a little before midnight, and in a fit of rage or maybe out of jealousy, Garrison, who they portrayed as an angry, impassioned killer, repeatedly stabbed Miss Bradshaw to death. Not content with just stabbing her, he pounced on her defenseless prone body and continued to pummel her. A crime of unbridled passion.

The prosecution painted Garrison as an insanely jealous person who had previously shouted at Hazel and her sister, Edith, alleging that Hazel saw other men on the side. That Hazel was seeing other men, particularly when she and Moss were broken up, was not contested. Edith recounted a time when Garrison called on Hazel unexpectedly and found Ted Williams making a hasty exit out the back door. No, not that Ted Williams, of baseball fame. He was only thirteen at the time, although he lived nearby. Twenty-three-year-old Teddy Williams worked as a stenographer at a local insurance agency and saw Hazel occasionally.

Was Garrison the livid, jealous suitor that Edith Bradshaw made him out to be? Perhaps he showed anger when confronting Hazel's other male friends. Both of Hazel's sisters, Edith and Bobbie, cited examples of his anger. As reported in the local press, one testified Garrison shouted at Hazel that "If I don't get her, no one else will. I'll kill her, sure as fate." At face value, there would be no reason for the sisters to lie. And the sailor guy felt threatened by Garrison, or so he said. Speaking of Hazel's jilted suitors, Cora had warned her daughter, "You're so pretty and men friends take it hard when they're disappointed." Garrison's coworkers and friends described him as mild-mannered, cordial, and even docile. But as we all know, sometimes the green-eyed monster springs from inside us. Crimes of passion are situational.

Fairchild elicited from both Mrs. Bradshaw and Edith that not only had Garrison eaten with the family, but he also had brought food to the home and helped prepare it. The defense went into great detail to trace the whereabouts of Hazel and Moss on that fateful night. Jurors learned they met downtown at around 5:30 and went to two movies. The first one at the Broadway, and a second one at the Superba on Third and C Streets. The Broadway screened two movies for twenty-five cents that evening, *The Third Alarm* with Anita Louise, and a second bill, *The Dancers* with Lois Moran. The total running time for both movies, with maybe a cartoon or newsreel and short intermission thrown in, would have been about two hours and thirty-five minutes.

If they went to the six o'clock screening, Moss and Hazel would have left the Broadway a little after eight thirty. They then walked the six blocks over to C Street to the Superba. Louis Lechien, a fellow who knew them both, testified he saw the couple downtown near Broadway at eight thirty. When asked about what color suit Garrison had on, a key issue for both the defense and the prosecution, he could not say for sure. Perplexed by that answer, Fairchild tried another tact. Asked by Fairchild if he noticed the girl more than Garrison, Lechien smiled and said yes. In fact, he said, his wife had told him to come along and stop looking at that girl. The gallery giggled softly.

After seeing *The Finger Points,* a movie depicting the corruption of the press with Richard Barthelmess, an upcoming young actor named Clark Gable, and Fay Wray, who would become famous in *King Kong* two years later, they left the Superba between 10:40 and 10:50. They then started the walk to her house, supposedly arriving there a bit before midnight.

The prosecution scoffed at that timing and said it took a police officer more than an hour and fifteen minutes to walk the same journey. An intrepid news reporter said it took him even longer, one hour and thirty-two minutes. Begging to differ, the defense offered the statement of a fifty-five-year-old man and a seventy-seven-year-old gent who said they walked the four miles in fifty-eight minutes—drawing some light laughter from the galley. Perhaps, it was suggested, the police officer and the reporter should frequent the gym more than the local bars and donut shops. To get a better idea of the time required to cover the four miles, I, no paragon of physical fitness, made the trek in almost exactly one hour. Although, admittedly, I did not have the company of a young woman in sensible shoes.

In a stunning blow to the prosecution, the defense called four witnesses, one of whom saw Garrison and Hazel after they emerged from Balboa Park and another near her home. A night watchman, Harry R. Stevenson, fifty years of age, told the Court that he saw Moss and Hazel as they passed the Plaza de Panama on the northwestern edge of the park near the large fountain on the west side of Park Boulevard. The couple then walked past the ornate carousel that stood silent for the night. Stevenson was precise in the time he saw the couple: it was 11:20.

Stevenson's testimony placed the couple on the northwest portion of the park but still south of the murder scene. The couple had made the walk from Third Avenue and C Street to the Plaza, nearly one point seven miles, in less than thirty minutes. That would be a rate of about three and a half miles per hour, certainly not leisurely and just short of a brisk pace. The July 31st *Union* stressed that Stevenson told the jury that "they were walking mighty fast." Remember Hazel's fortune-telling slip from the weight machine? Explaining the fast pace, Garrison said that he and Hazel were trying to lose weight and that she "insisted that the movement of hips from fast walking led to weight reduction."

More damning to the prosecution, the next witness, Curtis. L. Lowe testified he saw the couple several blocks north of and beyond the park along Park Boulevard, which would be approximately eight blocks from Hazel's home. Garrison himself testified that he and Hazel had passed a sandwich shop at Park and El Cajon Boulevard. He even sketched the seating arrangement of the four people they saw through the large plate-glass windows. Wanda and Raymond Connors, owners of the café, testified that they did not specifically remember seeing Hazel and Moss walk by. Asked if they saw anyone walk by their windows, they both replied that no, it was difficult to see out into the dark from the brightly lit café.

How about Garrison's sketch of customers in the café? Wanda and Raymond said, oh yes, the sketch appeared accurate for the few customers in their place a little before midnight. Attorney Fairchild drove home the point that unless Moss and Hazel turned around and went back into the park, they clearly had been seen beyond the scene of her death and well on the way safely to her house. Whatever man some witnesses might have said they saw by himself near the Indian Village could not have been his client.

A fourth defense witness, seventeen-year-old Walton Dobbs, sometimes referred to as Welton, described as a Negro youth by the *Sacramento Bee* and as a colored youth or colored boy in the *Tribune* and *Union,* told the jury he clearly saw the pair even closer to Hazel's home, only a few blocks from the Bradshaw house a little before midnight. He also testified that as he rode his motorcycle past a dark automobile near the Bradshaw house, the driver looked away and then rapidly drove off. This testimony shored up the defense's case that someone other than Garrison may have been with Hazel that late night or early morning. His mother, Mary Dobbs, a housekeeper and nurse in a nearby home at 4521 Alabama Street, offered even more explosive testimony. Mrs. Dobbs said she also saw a dark, square-backed sedan cruising around the Bradshaw house late that evening and in the early morning.

Leaning forward from the witness stand as if sharing a secret, Mrs. Dobbs informed the rapt jurors that, upon hearing about the murder, she had told Cora Bradshaw, Hazel's mother, about the mysterious auto. Mrs. Bradshaw sternly told Dobbs, "For God's sake, don't tell anyone else." Mrs. Bradshaw earlier denied giving such advice to Mary Dobbs.

Using the little more than one-hour walk home as a baseline, the defense stressed that Hazel and Moss had made it to the Panama Plaza at 11:20, then walked the approximately one and a half miles north to where Lowe saw them, and then finally a half mile farther to just a few blocks from the Bradshaw home at 4510 Alabama Street, where the Dobbs saw them a little before midnight. Allowing thirty minutes to walk the total of two miles would be reasonable, with a time between twenty-five minutes and thirty-five minutes being typical. Then, according to that scenario, Garrison briskly walked back to the streetcar line and caught the midnight Number 11 car.

On the witness stand, the Number 11 motorman, J.M. Hughes, verified that Garrison, whom he recognized from several previous fares, boarded the car at 12:10 at Park Boulevard and University Avenue, almost nine-tenths of a mile from Hazel's home. Hughes reiterated that Garrison "was not agitated in the least and I could not see from outward appearances that he had been involved in anything unusual." Portions of his testimony, however, had changed between the inquest and the trial, potentially harming his assertions.

At the previous pre-trial hearing in May, Hughes testified he could not remember if Garrison wore a tie when he boarded the streetcar. Yet, at trial, Hughes was certain that Garrison had been tieless. Fairchild, in his cross-examination, implied that the police had coerced Hughes into changing his testimony. Hughes denied that accusation, stating "I just remembered better the more time I had to think about it." Hughes testified that there was nothing mussed up or out of place on Mr. Garrison as far as he could notice, certainly not blood on his clothing.

Hughes said he noted a whiff of wine or other alcohol on Garrison's breath but assured jurors he was sober. In response, the prosecution produced one of Garrison's ties collected from his closet, a red-and-green affair with some apparent traces of blood—Hazel Bradshaw's blood, they loudly proclaimed with no evidence to that fact.

On cross-examination, county chemical specialist Ernst Mundkowski admitted he could not match the blood on Garrison's tie with Hazel's blood. When pressed on the determination that the tested substance was actually human blood, Mundkowski admitted his results were only presumptive for human blood, not absolute. *Presumptive* in this case meant there was simply a possibility that the substance on the tie was blood. Even then, the testing, if Mundkowski used phenolphthalein, would not have differentiated human from animal blood. Blood typing as a forensic technique was in its infancy in 1931. Comparing dried blood to determine blood type or even the actual presence of blood was still problematic until the FBI refined such testing in the early 1940s.

To further rebuke the tie testimony, the defense called Mrs. Mary Gailey, the motion picture ticket seller, who swore she remembered Garrison and Hazel purchasing movie tickets that night. She told the Court that she was sure that Moss "wore a blue-and-white striped necktie, as he testified, that night." Fairchild introduced as evidence a blue tie with a white stripe from Garrison's tie rack and Mrs. Gailey said, yes, that was the tie. When pressed by the defense, she indignantly insisted that she knew men's ties and Garrison's tie was certainly not red and green. And, as Fairchild sarcastically noted, while holding the tie up to the jurors, it was a bloodless tie at that.

When questioned by Fairchild about prosecutor Bristow's claim that Mundkowski had found human blood in the scrapings taken from under Garrison's fingernails, the nervous witness qualified his findings. He noted that actually the substance was only presumptive blood, but he could not determine if it was human or animal.

Okay, perhaps more testing could resolve the issue? asked Fairchild.

Well, Mundkowski slowly answered, looking nervously towards the prosecutors, he had used up the minute scrapings in his earlier test; none remained.

And what other substances were discovered in the fingernail scrapings? Fairchild inquired.

Mundkowski replied he did not know, "he was instructed only to test for blood."

Ohhh, I see, Fairchild slowly exclaimed as he turned towards the jury.

Later, in his own defense, Garrison told the jurors that while in jail, he was rarely given utensils to eat with. After three days in jail, a trustee had made him a medium-rare hamburger, which he ate with his hands just before submitting to tests by Mundkowski.

And, Mr. Garrison, how did you eat the hamburger? asked Fairchild.

"I ate it with my hands, and it was quite a mess," answered Garrison. The implication to the jury was that hamburger meat—perhaps especially medium-rare meat—would contain hemoglobin, which could be misidentified as blood.

There were also heated disputes over the color and type of suit that Garrison wore on that fateful evening. His landlady at the El Centro Apartments said she saw him about five o'clock, nicely dressed in a brown suit with a light-colored shirt. Yet a friend of Garrison said when he saw Garrison and loaned him two dollars at almost the same time downtown, he was wearing a blue serge suit, assumedly the same one he wore when he turned himself in to police the following morning.

Unable to score a knockout with the type or color of suit worn by Garrison the night of the murder, the prosecution tried another tact. Muir told the jurors that the oat spears found in the cuffs of Garrison's trousers were identical to those near the Indian Village crime scene. Fairchild scoffed at that assertion. A dry cleaner he called to the stand said probably sixty percent of men's trousers he processed had oat spears in their cuffs. Another witness said that without a very detailed study, one could not differentiate one field of wild oats from another. Later the jury foreman told a newsman that the *oat spear in the pants cuff* theory was ridiculous. He said, "All men get them there some time or another."

Going back to the night of the murder, the defense strongly suggested that Hazel had occasionally, and in particular on that night, entered a dark, older automobile driven by an unknown person at a late hour. Fairchild was careful to not throw shade on Hazel, suggesting only that she occasionally kept later hours with some unknown person or persons. Sitting in the gallery, Mrs. Bradshaw lowered her head and slowly shook it from side to side. Furthering the possibility that Hazel had late-night suitors, an invalid neighbor of the Bradshaws', who, it was implied, sat by her front window much of the time, told the Court that she often saw Hazel come and go in autos late at night.

Fairchild's approach verged on blaming the victim for her after-hours rendezvous leading to her death. Maybe even impugning her "clean and moral" status maintained by her mother and the prosecution. That possible aspersion aside, such late-night assignations after leaving Garrison may also explain her fatal movements the night she died. The specter of an unknown suitor in an automobile might explain Hazel's death, or at least the discovery of her body in Balboa Park.

The testimonies of Mrs. Dobbs and her son, coupled with that of McCue, were crucial in providing credence to the "other man" theory. Without their testimony, Fairchild's claim of another suitor would be baseless, sheer conjecture. Of course, the testimony of the neighborhood busybody helped too. To the jury, it must have seemed like the words of a distraught, protective mother against testimony from seemingly objective bystanders. In a time of shifting mores and a loosening of old scriptures, young men and women may have slipped out of the house at late hours--who knew?

To further sway the jurors from believing that Garrison was the only possible suspect, Fairchild called Walter Hamm, a coworker of Hazel, to the witness stand. Hamm, an older married man who sometimes gave Hazel a ride home, testified that someone had called Hazel at work and threatened her, but he offered no clue who the person might have been, except he overheard her several times say *Harry*. When the prosecutor asked Garrison who he thought killed Hazel, he answered either a sailor boy or the mysterious Harry. The defense hoped that Hamm's testimony, along with the dark sedan scenario, would at least get the jurors to entertain the idea of another plausible suspect, thus raising reasonable doubt.

Moss told the Court that there were at least two men who might have wanted to harm Hazel. Men he did not know, but one was a sailor whom Hazel might have spurned, and the second man was Harry, about whom he could not offer any details beyond what Mr. Hamm had offered. Moss told the jurors that he dearly loved Hazel and had no reason to harm her. Sure, they had a few lover's spats over the months they dated, but, he asked, doesn't every couple? There were nods of agreement in the jury box.

One seemingly powerful piece of evidence used by the prosecution, and touted in news accounts, was two cuts on Moss's hand that they theorized he incurred during the well-documented death struggle. The prosecution pointed out Garrison's injured hand must have resulted from the poor girl's hopeless fight for life. Further, the police testified that upon examination of his trousers while in jail, they noted a ripped-out right front pocket and rear hip pocket. And apparent blood residue remained on the remnant linings. This, the prosecution explained, proved that after stabbing Hazel, Garrison tried to remove the telltale blood smears from his hands.

To explain the otherwise incriminating cuts on Garrison's hand, the defense called to the stand a couple of Moss's poker buddies who testified that when they played poker with him prior to the night of the murder, he had bandages on his hand from a cut he suffered at work cutting bread. He did, they also pointed out, work in the commissary after all. Perhaps to further personalize Garrison to the jury and to dispel their thoughts about the scar, Fairchild walked Moss to the jury box and had him hold out his hands for all to inspect. Jurors nodded and murmured amongst themselves.

Regarding the missing pocket linings, Garrison testified that there was not a first-aid kit or bandages near his commissary workstation. In desperation to staunch the blood flow, which was not actually severe, he tore out portions of his pockets and wound the cloth around his right index finger. A supervisor at the railroad commissary vouched for the lack of bandages in the commissary. Fairchild also introduced the fact that the so-called "missing pockets" had not been noticed until the third day of Garrison's incarceration. Intake forms stated his clothing had been carefully combed. In court, Garrison testified that the police only patted him down and checked for a gun.

On July 27th, amidst a record-tying heat wave (the San Diego high temperature was eighty-four degrees that day, tying a forty-year-old record), the trial continued. Ceiling fans and large circular floor fans moved warm air around the stuffy courtroom. The defense brought two other sets of evidence to bolster their case. Both cast doubt on the police work and the coroner's report. Monte Clark, private investigator and supposed fingerprint specialist, testified that several days after the murder he lifted a bloody palm print from a wooden box at the crime scene. Why, he asked rhetorically, had the police not taken the box into evidence or at least lifted a print from it?

Clark said that the print did not match those of Garrison and that the prosecution had been remiss in not even gathering the box from the murder scene to examine. What other evidence had they missed, mused Clark? In rebuttal, the prosecution's expert fingerprint witness, Mr. Barlow, completely discounted Clark's thesis. He stated, perhaps accurately, that it was impossible to get a clean print from such a rough wooden surface. But the prosecution had perhaps planted doubt about the police investigation in the minds of the jurors. Perhaps even reasonable doubt about the guilt of Garrison.

The second evidentiary approach of the defense called into question the time of death. Fairchild called the former, and somewhat controversial, San Diego County Coroner Schuyler C. Kelly to testify as to the approximate time of Hazel's death. The prosecution objected, stating that Kelly was not a formally trained doctor and had retired from whatever standing he once maintained before the Court. Judge Turrentine excused the jurors and allowed Fairchild and Bristow to present their arguments to him. The judge said he would allow Kelly's testimony on the condition that Fairchild not imply that his witness was a city official or that he held a medical degree.

Under oath and the watchful eye of the judge, Kelly said he had conducted over six thousand autopsies, including one hundred and forty-nine homicides. Pressing his point, he told the Court he was well versed in the stages of rigor mortis and the variables of heat and cold on a dead human. Kelly, you might remember, had searched on his own the canyons near Virginia Brooks' home, hoping to discover where she had lain for more than a month after her death.

Contradicting the coroner's official report on Hazel Bradshaw, Kelly stunned the courtroom by stating that based on his over thirteen years of experience, Hazel's body, when studied at two o'clock on the afternoon of her discovery was in only a moderate stage of rigor, not even close to the full final stage.

Kelly confidently asserted that she died sometime between seven and ten in the morning. Fairchild cleverly left unsaid, for the moment, that they had noted earlier that Hazel's watch had stopped at 9:43. Later, he called to the witness stand a local watchmaker who testified that a blow from the knife, which was obviously to the watch, had broken a jewel and immediately stopped the watch. The implication of death in the morning hours on Sunday was that someone had killed her elsewhere—possibly in an auto and then dumped over or pulled through the Indian Village wall shortly afterwards. Sunrise was about 6 a.m. and between that time and roughly 6:30, lingering darkness would have at least partially shrouded dumping a body in a rarely trafficked area.

The defense also tied Garrison's testimony to the proposed time of death. Garrison testified that he and Hazel had each eaten a candy bar, had a bag of popcorn, and shared some peanuts while at the movies. He did not state specifically at which theater they had the snacks or at what time. To add a physical element and visual image to the story of the snacks, Fairchild introduced candy bars similar to those remnants found in Hazel's purse, but not in her stomach. Garrison testified that yes, those were the brands. The bars were passed amongst the jurors for inspection.

The coroner's report stated that Hazel's stomach contained no food. Indicating that her last food intake had been completely digested and moved on to the intestines prior to death. The rate at which a person digests food varies depending on the type of food and the exertion of a healthy person post-meal. Popcorn and peanuts, which are high in fiber, digest much slower than most foods, such as candy bars.

A San Diego County physical forensic specialist, while qualifying their estimate, told me that the popcorn and peanuts would have required approximately three hours to pass from the stomach. If the candy, nuts, and popcorn were consumed sometime between the first movie at eight o'clock and the last movie near ten o'clock, it is unlikely that Hazel's stomach would have been fully empty if she had been murdered before midnight. The implication from the lack of stomach contents and from the state of rigor mortis is that Hazel's murder occurred well after midnight when Garrison was riding home on the streetcar or already home in bed, maybe for several hours.

As the trial rapidly wound to a conclusion, both sides opted for a field trip. On July 30th, the jury, courtroom officials, and the press left the courthouse in the early morning to visit the crime scene in Balboa Park. Judge Turrentine said such a venture was dangerous in that it might allow jurors to talk amongst themselves or to compare notes. He admonished them not to do so and instructed court bailiffs, if they saw such actions, to intervene.

Traveling by bus, the jurors and judge retraced the route taken by Moss and Hazel, and drove past the faux Indian Village. They stopped where the boys found Hazel, viewed the sandwich shop near the corner of Park Boulevard and University Avenue, where Garrison said they saw late-night diners and stood in front of the Bradshaw home on Alabama Street. They then drove past the home of McCue, who said he saw a young woman get into a dark automobile at half past midnight on the night of the murder.

Garrison, his attorney, his brother, the prosecution, and others made the trek by automobile. At the request of the defense, the jurors entered the home where Mrs. Dobbs said she could look out the window and see the Bradshaw home. It was there she saw a young woman get into an auto. As noted by reporters, despite what the prosecution had told the jurors in the courtroom, the view from the Dobbs' home was direct and clear to the Bradshaw home. The prosecution maintained that someone had cut the trees back since the night of the murder, allowing a better view. Cut back by whom? Fairchild queried. Receiving no answer, Fairchild simply smiled.

It was a hot, cloudless day in the low eighties and several of the men shed their jackets. A morning marine layer was just retreating off the coast. The three bailiffs and Moss Garrison kept their jackets on throughout the excursion. Newspaper reporters captured the entire event, noting the sober mood of all the attendees and the continued composure of Garrison. Photographers dutifully took shots of the Bradshaw home.

Returning to the courtroom, Judge Turrentine told the jurors that after a brief break, he would call for closing arguments from both sides. He cautioned the prosecution and the defense that each had only three hours to close out. When the Court reconvened at two in the afternoon, a near riot broke out as spectators jockeyed for seats and standing room at the rear of the courtroom. Over two hundred people tried to cram themselves into a room that could hold only one hundred people. While being pushed aside, one elderly man, loudly claiming his rights as a taxpayer, struck a court officer with his cane. Bailiffs restored order and refused the crowd entrance once the room filled up. The judge gaveled the court to order and warned the seated and standing spectators he would clear the room if there were further disturbances. The room remained restless but orderly for the duration.

Chapter Thirteen

"Justice Never Required the Sacrifice of a Victim"

In his hour and fifteen-minute closing argument, as covered in the July 31st *Union*, prosecutor Sam Bristow began by telling the jury, "Circumstantial evidence is the most dependable kind of proof, because it cannot lie." This statement was an attempt to discredit the defense's eyewitnesses, such as Mrs. Dobbs and others. The message to the jury was to disregard what people thought they saw in the night; we have hard evidence that is irrefutable.

To follow that up, prosecutor Oran Muir verged on hyperbole when he told the jury, "This murder was the most beastly and cruel ever committed in San Diego." He also justified the circumstantial nature of the evidence before them by noting that many murders have only such evidence and most lack eyewitnesses.

Both Bristow and Muir were correct in pointing out the unreliability of eyewitnesses, although at the time, they did not view such witnesses with as jaundiced an eye as they often are now.

The prosecution pushed a purported motive for such a violent stabbing as that of a spurned lover—in this case, the "fiend" Garrison. One witness for the prosecution testified that he saw Garrison and Bradshaw quarreling downtown around nine o'clock. Bristow called Garrison "a beast with an uncontrollable temper." He argued that the defense did not offer any valid arguments beyond confused timelines, mysterious auto rides from shadowy suitors, and contradictory witnesses. Bristow called the defense a "patchwork of lies and conjecture."

Bristow noted Garrison took the stand and, in Bristow's view, told a good story but lied. Bristow approached the jury box, pacing up and down along the edge of the worn wooden rail. He looked the jurors in their eyes and softly said that Garrison can lie all he wants but "Hazel's lips are forever sealed." Stepping forward as Bristow seated himself, Prosecutor Muir said he, however, could speak for Hazel.

In a final impassioned statement, Muir told the jury, "If Hazel reached home the defendant didn't kill her. But if not, then the defendant is guilty. When you find him guilty, you have done only half of your duty. I ask you, now by your verdict to sentence the defendant to hang by the neck until he is dead." Clearly, the prosecution was banking on the idea that they had proved beyond a doubt that Hazel never stepped on her porch that night. She did not close the screen door; her little dog did not greet her. No, instead, she was viciously murdered by Garrison several miles from home.

Defense attorney Fairchild offered a vastly different narrative. In his closing argument for the defense, Fairchild hammered on the possibility of an unindicted killer or killers in a dark automobile. Killers that the police failed to pursue. Or perhaps it was another unindicted, jilted lover, one of those mysterious sailors who hung around Hazel, or maybe, just maybe, the shadowy Harry? Why haven't we heard more about him from the prosecution? Fairchild rhetorically queried.

Noting that the police had a string of unsolved murders on their hands, Fairchild suggested perhaps they needed to solve one. No matter that it led to the conviction and hanging of an innocent man. He also said there was no evidence that Hazel and Moss were actually at odds—hadn't they just spent the evening together, gone to not one but three movies? Fairchild stressed the timeline and solid witnesses, not circumstantial evidence. Evidence that proved Garrison was on a streetcar and far away from the murder scene, or already at home in bed when poor Hazel had met her death after midnight or in the early morning of Sunday. Take your pick on the hour of death, Fairchild exclaimed, Garrison was not at the scene!

Fairchild reminded the jury that Garrison had contacted the police immediately upon finding out about the murder—hardly, he said, the actions of a guilty man. And finally, he noted the absence of forensic evidence tying his client to the murder. No footprints, no fingerprints, no murder weapon, no verified human blood on his client's clothes. No blood at his home, no scratches on his face or arms, and no real motive. Turning prosecutor Bristow's fiery tirade back on him, Fairchild asked the jury to inspect his client. Did the diminutive, soft-spoken Southerner look like a vicious killer, a beast, to them? He answered for them: of course not.

Fairchild then made a challenging move by suggesting possible mistakes made by the police, particularly ex-Captain Hayes. *The Ogden Standard-Examiner* called Fairchild's derision of the police "a vicious attack upon the San Diego police department." Why, he asked, were neighbors of the Bradshaws not more thoroughly interviewed? Why was Mr. McCue not officially summoned to the inquest so he could mention the dark sedan? Who was the mysterious Harry? Why hadn't the police searched for him?

Well, because. as Fairchild later told the press, ex-Captain Paul J. Hayes was not interested in gathering actual evidence. As he himself had said, he "placed little importance to McCue's story." Fairchild turned to Captain Hayes seated in the gallery. Pointing directly towards him, he said, "he knew that this little defendant was not guilty, but he had to convict someone."

The July 31st *Tribune* reported that as Hayes angrily twisted in his chair, Fairchild doubled down, reminding the jury that when the case started, "Hayes was about to retire, there had been four murders here and he was in a desperate situation. He wanted to try this little defendant because they knew he was helpless." Standing in front of Hayes, the *Tribune* said Fairchild shook his head and slowly said Hayes "knew that this defendant wasn't guilty."

Why, asked Fairchild, did Mrs. Bradshaw not want Mary Dobbs to mention that dark car on the street? Were her assurances about not hearing Hazel come into the house just an explanation for falling asleep at that late hour? Fairchild said that the police "made no effort to find the real murderer." Instead, they were trying to "convict this poor innocent defendant." The July 31st *Tribune* reported that pacing back and forth before the jury box, a highly animated Fairchild, "in his shirtsleeves, was dripping with perspiration, and his shirt was streaked with wet spots as he passionately shouted, 'you can do nothing less but acquit the defendant.'" He rested his defense.

As a standard practice at the beginning of homicide trials, the prosecution and the defense are allowed to submit to the judge what they believe should be the judge's instructions to the jury before jury deliberation. Today, the State of California has an approved model for such instructions to standardize the script and to reduce appeals based on judicial irregularities, but in 1931, judges had much more latitude. Amongst the few extant subpoenas, warrants, and other documents on file at the San Diego Superior Court archives from the Garrison trial, Fairchild's version of his request for jury instructions is insightful. Fairchild hoped the judge would tell the jurors that

> the burden of proof in this case is at all times upon
> the People to prove the guilt of the defendant to
> your satisfaction beyond a reasonable doubt. The

defendant is not required to prove his innocence. It is your duty to act with the greatest of caution; it is safer to err in acquitting and better that many guilty persons should escape, than that one innocent man should suffer, justice never required the sacrifice of a victim. Unless you are satisfied from all of the evidence in this case beyond a reasonable doubt that the defendant killed Hazel Bradshaw as alleged in the information, you should return a verdict of not guilty.

Judge Turrentine rejected Fairchild's submittal. We do not know what the instructions to the jury were, but they probably stressed reasonable doubt and the value of circumstantial evidence. Judge Turrentine may also have stressed that it was, in fact, and in jurisprudence, the state's responsibility to prove guilt, not the defense's obligation to prove innocence.

The jury convened at 2:45 p.m. to consider the fate of Moss Garrison. They left the stifling courtroom, walked a short distance down the hall, and entered the room marked as JURORS ONLY. At 4:40 that afternoon, the verdict was in. Before the verdict was read, Judge Turrentine ordered the courtroom emptied except for court officials, the principals in the trial, and news reporters. Deliberation lasted less than two hours. Unanimous votes—NOT GUILTY. Recorded in Superior Court as Verdict #67815, the decision gave Moss Garrison his freedom. Then the public quickly returned to the courtroom. Some observers seemed stunned, but most nodded their heads in agreement and smiled at Moss Garrison.

Jury foreman J. Russell Jones told the *Tribune* that there were two ballots, although the first one was what he called "a feeler" just to gauge jurors' sentiments. The second, more official ballot, like the first, was unanimous for acquittal. Foreman Jones also added, "Coming fresh into the trial, not knowing anything about the case or knowing anyone involved, I couldn't see any reasons for the case even coming to trial." He described the prosecution's efforts as a patchwork of conjectures with little substantial evidence. Others on the jury expressed similar sentiments. Some faulted the police directly, and some said they just could not believe that Moss could do such a terrible deed. Another juror said that except for a motive based on jealousy, the prosecution proved virtually nothing.

J. Russell Jones, a self-proclaimed God-fearing man, further remarked, "I had no idea that Garrison was the little, gentle sort of man he appeared to be. We were fully convinced that Garrison took Hazel Bradshaw home that night." In a very real sense, the jury took the prosecution's statement that if they believed Hazel made it home, Garrison should be acquitted, to heart. Several days later, some jurors told reporters that members of the clergy and well-positioned people called them to thank them for making the right decision. The press did not report any backlash against Garrison.

Holding audience with the assembled newspaper reporters, Foreman Jones pointed a finger at a person of some other ethnic group as more likely to have killed Hazel. He told reporters, "The knife doesn't seem, to me, to be the American way of doing away with a person. It smacks more of the southern European or Oriental method." Jones said that he and some other jurors thought that it would have taken a powerful man or men to throw or carry Hazel's body into the enclosure, not a small person such as Garrison.

Some jurors expressed concern that while Garrison sat in jail being investigated and then dragged through the trial, the actual murderer walked the streets—just as the killers of that poor little Brooks girl and Louise Teuber's killer still did. That's right, they told reporters, he walked the streets with the other killer or killers of young women. They demanded to know what, if anything, the police and district attorney were doing regarding that. Or, as the *Sacramento Bee* newspaper said about the not-guilty verdict, "The brutal murder of Hazel Bradshaw to-day was added to the long list of unsolved murders of San Diego." In truth, Moss Garrison joined the approximately eighty percent of acquitted accused murderers in the early 1900s. Many found freedom because of inadequate or shoddy police work, lack of solid forensic evidence, and rushes to judgment.

Upon hearing the verdict, a relieved Garrison smiled, slowly strode over to the jury box, and shook hands with each of the jurors, including the three women who reportedly had tears running down their powdered and rouged cheeks. *The San Diego Evening Tribune,* clearly hoping for an explosion of emotion, reported in bold headlines that "GARRISON REMAINS STOIC SILENCE EVEN AFTER VERDICT RETURNED FREEING HIM IN BRADSHAW DEATH." The paper compared him to a nonplussed cigar store wooden Indian. Garrison's release from custody shared the news with dairies being blown up in what was known as the Milk Wars. Thomas Edison was on his deathbed, and yet another body was found floating in San Diego Bay. Moss Garrison, finally a free man after over two and a half months in jail, steadfastly refused to give the press fodder for their sensationalist verbal cannons.

When queried by a *Union* reporter about his future plans, Garrison simply said that they had promised him his job back at the commissary and that "I am going to lie round for a week or so to get back my strength. My old job waits for me." According to extant court documents, four days later, the Court returned his trousers with the ripped-out pockets to him. Strangely, it would be, for some unknown reason, a month before Hazel's purse and watch were given to her sister Bobbie.

For once, retired Captain Hayes and the police offered no interviews. They apparently had no plan B to search for a killer and provided no details of possible further investigations. For all intents and purposes, the case was closed. Soon, the newspapers also fell silent on the search for Hazel's killer. The August 1st *Sacramento Bee* weighed in noting that, "The brutal murder of Hazel Bradshaw today was added to the long list of unsolved murders of San Diego, a city which witnessed so far this year the slaying of a 10-year-old girl and three women." The out-of-town newspaper could not resist adding that the Bradshaw case was the only one of the several murders that had even seen the inside of a courtroom.

Defense attorney Fairchild was not as stoic as his client. In follow-up interviews with the press that appeared in both the *Tribune* and *Union* on August 1st, he railed against Hayes and his investigators. He said that "Hayes did not want to expose evidence that might be favorable to the defendant" and may have even hidden important evidence. Fairchild may have had a point. In 1931, police and district attorneys could keep or not disclose evidence that they believed might not help their case. Keep in mind that it would not be until *Brady v. Maryland* in 1970 that prosecutors were legally obligated to provide exculpatory evidence to the defense as part of the discovery process.

Fairchild further opined that they forced his client to prove himself innocent "rather than the prosecutor being called upon to prove him guilty" as is expected in American jurisprudence. As reported in the August 14th *Los Angeles Times*, Garrison and his attorney threatened to sue the city of San Diego, claiming that he had been deprived of his civil rights and treated poorly while in custody. Weeks later they brought suit, but after an unfavorable preliminary hearing, Garrison and Fairchild dropped the suit and moved on with their lives. Months later, Fairchild defended Marta Marin against charges that she violated the Volstead Act and knowingly produced and sold illegal alcohol. In the public notice of her trial, readers were reminded that Fairchild had recently gained a not-guilty verdict for Garrison. Marin pleaded to lesser charges and paid a small fine.

With the acquittal of Garrison and with no other viable suspects, the murder of Hazel Bradshaw rapidly became a cold case. It is likely that if the police and district attorney had not so rapidly focused on Garrison, more suspects may have been investigated. The case could have had a different, more just outcome, or not. Instead, Miss Bradshaw joined Virginia Brooks, Louise Teuber, and several others as San Diego's unsolved murders of 1931.

In January 1932, six months after Garrison's acquittal, John MacDonald, a convicted car thief and ex-speakeasy owner, told San Diego police an extraordinary tale. The January 11th and 12th *Tribune* called MacDonald's story farfetched. He said a drunken patron at his gin joint in Santa Monica had told a drinking buddy he knew who killed Hazel Bradshaw. The man alleged that the killer was a woman who murdered Hazel in a fit of rage and jealousy. MacDonald also told the police that the female murderer had fled the country.

When queried regarding the new theory of a female killer, Moss Garrison told the press, "I don't know who the girl this fellow speaks of might be, as I don't give a continental about anyone but Hazel." Garrison said, however, that he had tried to trace the story of a downtown San Diego drunk who while inebriated, told a hotel clerk Hazel died at the hands of a jealous woman. Whether this drunk informant was the same person mentioned by MacDonald is unclear. Captain Kelly of the San Diego police half-heartedly followed up those improbable leads, but they proved to be fruitless—at least to the police department.

Hazel Bradshaw's murder would occasionally pop up in a news report over the next few decades, but with no resolution to her death. In a retrospective newspaper piece on Balboa Park's War Memorial Building that sits almost on Hazel's murder site, an April 1967, *San Diego Union* article mentioned in passing the unsolved murder of Hazel Bradshaw there over thirty years before.

Did the murderers of the three unfortunate girls ever kill again? If we assume that both Hazel Bradshaw and Louise Teuber were killed in crimes of passion, then probably not. If Hazel was murdered out of jealousy or on a late-night date gone very wrong, then the killer may have ultimately settled into a law-abiding life of normalcy. For Louise's killer, if he was Herman Newby, there is no evidence that he killed again, only that he terrorized his second wife, assaulted at least one person, and molested his daughter. If someone else killed Louise, we are left to speculate that they did not repeat their crime. Or at least not in a way that research has uncovered.

The person who killed Virginia Brooks is a somewhat different situation. If we believe statistics that pedophiles rarely kill their victims, then Virginia's killer may have, and presumably did, continue to prey on children—he may or may not have killed again. Of the three murders, that of Virginia is the one most possibly linked to what we today label as a serial killer. Beginning with Virginia in 1931 and extending into 1935, more than five children between the ages of seven and sixteen were kidnapped and murdered in San Diego. That raises the specter of a serial child molester and killer in San Diego. No one was ever tried for those atrocities either.

Besides Garrison's reported run-in with the law for gambling, were any of the suspected killers arrested for other crimes? Cyril Smith, a strong possibility in Louise Teuber's murder, was convicted late in life of sexual crimes. Did the three killers, whoever they were, die natural deaths or meet some other end? Can we even consider that the failure to imprison the killers led to more deaths? Following his morals conviction, Herman Newby had small run-ins with the law back East but nothing substantial. We know how Herman died, but if he was not Louise's killer, then what of the actual murderer? Perhaps, if the killers were young men in 1931, the murderers used their lethal skills and fought in World War II, maybe even with valor, or met their own demise in a foreign land. Or….?

AFTERWORD

It is a strange and fascinating journey to follow the life arcs of the three murdered young women and persons associated with them in life and death. At the end of it all, you come to know a great deal about the people, the places, the legal system (then and now), and the times. So much is familiar and yet so much is foreign.

San Diego has undergone terrific growth since the three tragic murders in 1931. Today, blocky apartments and medical buildings have replaced the Brooks home, and most of the other residences. University Avenue and Virginia's route along it now supports a hodgepodge of small stores. Many of the storefronts are ethnic. Automotive repair shops and even some storefront churches would greet Virginia today. Virginia's elementary school, although remodeled to include security measures, still sits on a slight hill above University Avenue. Kids her age file through the doors with book bags and lunches. The Egyptian Garage, a listed historic landmark that she regularly walked past, is home to a liquor store and auto shop.

The lonely mesa where the body of little Virginia was discovered is now part of Marine Corps Air Station Miramar. Where the *Spirit of St. Louis* once went through its air trials, supersonic jets now roar into the sky and, of course, portions of *Top Gun* were filmed there. The gunny sack drop site is four hundred fifty yards east of I-15, north of Highway 52, and southeast of the eastern terminus of Miramar Way. The little community of Miramar is long gone and virtually erased from history. Miramar Mesa itself, in this area east of the freeway, remains unchanged. Sage and scrub still cloak the flat and undeveloped land. A natural pavement of small cobbles provides a thin veneer over the hard reddish subsurface soils.

Game trails used by rabbits and the occasional deer crisscross the cobbled mesa. It is easy to imagine the scene of the discovery of Virginia's body decades ago. George Moses, the man who stumbled across her body, stayed in San Diego for at least another decade picking up odd jobs here and there. A self-described loner, he never married, and in 1950, aged sixty-nine, he was living in a low-rent boarding house in Los Angeles. The federal census noted he listed himself as "unable to work."

The Wahlstrom property where Harry Wahlstrom was taken into custody as a prime suspect is now in the cleared right-of-way immediately east of the northbound 805 freeway. The Owen Hayes home on Altadena, where Dennis Stroud said he supposedly heard Hayes' confess to accidentally killing Virginia Brooks, was replaced by one of many ubiquitous stucco apartments in the area.

In Ocean Beach, the little cottage at 5065 ½ Brighton Avenue, from where Mrs. Helen Clough and her companions were taken in for questioning, is virtually unchanged. The little bungalow home of Virginia's mother, Blanche, from where she was rushed to the county hospital and died, still stands at 3728 Marlborough Avenue.

Virginia rests in a burial plot at Mount Hope Cemetery next to her mother. Recently, Virginia's niece, Rowena Lux, told me that the family never really got over the tragedy. The kidnapping and murder ordeal, along with the two deaths, tore the family apart. Rowena's father, George Melvin Brooks, Virginia's younger brother, died in 2005, seventy-four years after the murder of his sister. In going through his belongings, the family found a creased, dry and yellowed news clipping describing his sister's murder in his worn wallet. For some, closure never comes.

Nellie (Newby) Brown, the mother of Herman Newby, and whose son is the person whom I would still consider a prime suspect in Teuber's murder, lived a long life with her second husband Francis Brown in (strangely enough, my hometown) Anderson, Indiana. The Browns took part in local activities, including membership in the same Methodist church as my grandparents. Nellie died in 1948 and Francis lived another thirteen years, dying in 1961. Diane Powe, Herman's daughter from a second marriage, who graciously provided invaluable information and photos, is alive and living in Texas. I cannot thank her enough for the information and photos she provided.

The two theaters where Moss Garrison and Hazel Bradshaw spent the evening of May 2, watching the flickering screens were demolished years ago. The Panama Plaza Fountain, where the night watchman saw Hazel and Moss stroll by, still shoots streams of frothy water into the air. Not far away, the ornate carousel continues its endless circular orbit to the amusement of young children. The brass ring remains like justice, oftentimes elusive. To the north just off Park Boulevard and a little south of Roosevelt Middle School is a grassy area next to the War Memorial Building where my buddies and I played football on Sunday mornings in the 1960s. In the War Memorial Building itself, we danced to "Angel Baby" by Rosie and the Originals. Out in the parking lot we fought with boys from Hoover High School; we usually won. Fifty yards to the west is where the two boyhood chums, Richard and Jess, found Hazel's bloody body.

The so-called Indian Village and the wall behind which Hazel's body was hidden are long gone. The village lives on only in sepia-toned postcards of the time. Richard Charles Roehl and Jess Alfred Zimmerman, the small boys who discovered Hazel's body, grew to be over six feet tall, married, and fathered children of their own. One wonders if they ever told the story of that very special Sunday morning to their children. The Bradshaw home at 4510 Alabama Street still stands and the tracks of the streetcar that her accused killer rode home that fateful night still exists. Albeit buried beneath layers of asphalt along Park Boulevard, where they are occasionally unearthed by construction crews. Cora Bradshaw stayed in San Diego and no doubt continued to believe, as do other family members to this day, that Moss Garrison brutally murdered her daughter and got off scot-free. Cora lived to be eighty-eight, passing away thirty-eight years after her daughter.

Harry Carr, the *Los Angeles Times* pundit who poked satire at the befuddled San Diego police detectives, died five years after Hazel, but not before receiving a nomination for a Pulitzer Prize. Police Officer Jerry Lightner, one of the first on the Hazel Bradshaw scene, died six years after the discovery from pneumonia. Abijah Fairchild, Garrison's skilled attorney, continued to practice law for less than a decade after his most famous, or infamous, trial. He died in 1940.

The homes in the 3400 block of Park Boulevard just north of Upas Street, where Hazel and Moss continued their journey after leaving Balboa Park, are much as they were in 1931—but far more expensive now. Someone looking out their picture windows today could easily imagine the couple briskly walking north towards University Avenue in the late night.

Moss Garrison, the soft-spoken suspect in Hazel's murder, stayed in California for several years. In fact, his employer, Santa Fe Railway, as promised gave him his old commissary job back after his acquittal. In 1935, he was arrested on a misdemeanor charge of patronizing a gambling establishment downtown. Probably with some justification, he claimed police harassment. By 1940, Moss was living in Miami, Florida, where he would spend the rest of his life. Over the next two decades, he had a variety of jobs, including steam presser, warehouseman, and laborer. Moss died in Miami in September 1966.

Carson Aaron Garrison, loyal brother of Moss Garrison, spent the rest of his life in the Orange County and Los Angeles area with his wife Estrella. Carson owned his own garage at times, where he serviced automobiles. At other times, he worked for garage owners as a mechanic and electrician.

Prosecutor Oran Muir fell ill while prosecuting a case in 1934 and died a year later. Captain Paul J. Hayes, who seemed hellbent on convicting Moss Garrison, died in 1947. The intrepid Deputy Sheriff Lieutenant Blake Mason, who worked both the Brooks case and the Teuber case, left law enforcement and became Captain of San Diego lifeguards in the late 1940s. After retirement, Mason suffered heart issues in the 1960s and died in November 1967 following heart surgery.

Dr. Elliott Colby, the autopsy surgeon for Hazel, continued in private practice. He and his wife Harriet were members of San Diego's semi-elite social set. He served as president of the Kiwanis and raised money for Camp Fire Girls. She hosted many parties and benefits for children's causes. Throughout his career, Dr. Colby was often at odds with the sheriff's department over the cause of death for several people. The sheriff, and occasionally the police department, made sometimes unfounded findings of accidental deaths, which Dr. Colby refuted through forensic analysis.

In a highly controversial case in 1933, Dr. Colby strongly asserted that the death of Dalbert Aposhian, a seven-year boy found in the Bay, was a vicious murder. He reported the boy had been sexually assaulted and mutilated. In a touch of irony, Monte Clark, the self-proclaimed private investigator from the Hazel Bradshaw case, worked closely with the San Diego police to prove accidental death for the boy. At the time, many law enforcement officers and members of the public thought the police were involved in a coverup involving a wealthy Mission Hills family and their "degenerate" son. Dr. Colby, who held the rank of captain in the reserves, went on active duty in the US Army in 1940, and served in World War II having already served in World War I. Colby, who ultimately rose to the rank of colonel in the army reserve, died in 1960 at the age of sixty-three.

Mary Dobbs, the African American nurse and housekeeper who told jurors she had seen a black sedan near the Bradshaw home, lived a long life, dying in 1979. One of her daughters, Mildred Elaine, graduated with honors from San Diego High School in 1937. The same school attended by Louise Teuber six years before. Mildred went into nursing. One of Mrs. Dobbs' sons, Felix, enlisted in the army one month after Pearl Harbor, serving his country with distinction. There are plenty of Dobbs' descendants, but apparently no one remembers anything about the Bradshaw murder. Or the key role their ancestor played in the Garrison trial. For most, that is old forgotten history. They do, however, have a special place in their hearts for Miss Mary Dobbs.

Although Chief Investigator Clarence Morrill did not spend a great deal of time on the Brooks and Teuber cases and could not solve the murders, he continued his pursuit of criminals until his death from circulatory disorders in February 1940. Through his efforts, the California Bureau of Investigation made significant advances in using scientific forensics, including fingerprinting, blood analysis, crime scene preservation, and handwriting analysis.

His son, Sherwood Morrill, followed in his father's footsteps and became a well-known handwriting specialist and criminologist in his own right. Sherwood's most famous case work was in verifying and matching the handwriting on several letters and notes from the infamous Zodiac killer in

California. He is featured in the 2007 movie *Zodiac,* where he is played by Phillip Baker Hall. The Burns Detective agency, founded by America's Sherlock Holmes, William J. Burns, is now the quite successful Securitas Security Services USA.

The friends and gang of Louise Teuber had lives that, while perhaps unremarkable, were fulfilling. Sometimes, they lived quite long, given an average life expectancy of fifty-five years. Had she not been murdered, Louise might have lived, as her friends did, well into the 1970s or 1980s.

Antonio Espinoza Martinez, the young man who discovered her body, lived to be eighty-one, passing in 1983. It is unlikely that in the sixty years after that terrible morning in Mission Gorge, Antonio ever forgot what he found. Aside from being a witness to tragedy, Antonio lived the American immigrant dream by raising a family, learning construction skills, and working his way up in the ranks at a Chula Vista company, where he worked for over four decades. In his lifetime, Antonio saw, and experienced, significant advances in civil rights. After being forced to send their children to a substandard school, the Mexican population of Lemon Grove successfully sued the school district for racial segregation and discrimination in 1930-31. Superior Court Judge Claude Chambers ruled Mexicans were always considered as "White" going back to the early days of California statehood and that regardless of racial categorization, the district could not legally or morally separate Mexican children from the general school population. Antonio's obituary in the newspaper noted his extensive family, including children and grandchildren.

After Louise's death, her good friend Myretta Farris continued for a while to work at the five-and-dime and then, true to her long-held dreams, attended San Diego Teacher's College (now San Diego State University) pursuing a degree in education. She graduated in 1935 with an A.B. in elementary and junior high teaching. Myretta lived briefly in Warner Springs, a small community famous for its hot springs in the mountains outside of San Diego. In 1937, she taught at the rural one room San Felipe School on the desert's edge off S-2, where she was the only teacher. In later years, Myretta married George F. Snyder, and they moved to Alpine, California, where she taught for over thirty years. When she died in 1986 at seventy-three, Myretta was, and still is, remembered as a loving mother of three boys and as a dedicated teacher. Loretta Othick, another of Louise's friends, got a job at the Mission Theater, where she and Louise and their chums sometimes went to movies. Loretta married Robert Bacon, the assistant manager.

Leslie Airhart, briefly a suspect in Louise's death, continued for several years to work at the San Diego Soda Works as a cider builder, a person who tends to the pressing and processing of raw ciders and vinegars. In December 1935, Leslie married Helen Spurgeon in Yuma, Arizona. Leslie and Helen lived most of their lives in San Diego. He died fifty years after Louise Teuber in May 1981 at age seventy-three.

Cyril Smith, the daring young pilot who took Louise and other young women on soaring flights above the city also lived out his life in the San Diego area. Two years after her murder, Smith was involved in a near-fatal motorcycle accident. He continued his interest in flying throughout his life and took employment as a skilled welder, aircraft worker, and aeronautics teacher. At the age of seventy-three years, he was indicted and pleaded guilty to two of ten counts of oral copulation with two female minors, lewd behavior, and possession of pornography. Smith served a short sentence for his crime. Cyril died at eighty-eight years of age in Lakeside, California.

The building where William Teuber cut hair at 1445 University Avenue still stands, although the façade has been severely altered and now houses a tailor and salon. The Teuber house at 4644 Vermont Street looks much as it did in 1931. It is easy to imagine Louise walking out of the front door that Saturday morning. If you park in Ralph's shopping center off University Avenue, which used to be the site of the old Sears store, and walk across the pedestrian bridge, the Teuber home is the first residence on your left. It is that front door that young Louise, bored and restless, closed behind her and never returned.

Herman Newby's home and photographic studio on Maryland Avenue has long ago been replaced by an unremarkable stucco apartment house. The General Garage downtown where he worked in 1922 is now part of the thriving and bustling India Street nightlife scene. The Newby cabin at Whispering Pines, where sixteen-year-old Louise posed nude at least once for him, still stands near Julian in the mountains east of San Diego. I stood in front of the cabin with David Lewis, a former owner, and could easily visualize Louise on the wooden deck. If only the pines might share a whisper with us.

The lover's grove and picnic spot on the flanks of Black (Cowles) Mountain where Louise's body was found is now part of the heavily used Mission Trails Regional Park. Near to the interpretive center, hikers, bicyclists, and dog walkers take the Oak Grove Loop pass the wooded area where Louise's neatly piled clothes once lay at the foot of her lifeless, nearly nude body. In the 1950s and 1960s, decades before the establishment of the park, neighborhood children were often warned to avoid the area where Louise hanged, lest they encounter the spirit of the "lost young woman." Who, they said, wandered the oak groves.

In one of the several historical ironies of writing this book, I remembered conducting archaeological studies of the hundreds of acres in the park, then owned by the Kaiser-Dente Company. It was the 1970s and they had done some mining and rock quarrying on the hillsides and hoped to build yet another cookie-cutter community. Reflecting back on that project, I vividly remember having lunch under the shade of the oak trees in a little oak grove—pretty sure now that it was an outer edge of the grove that partially hid Louise Teuber's body forty years before. The development fell through, and government agencies purchased the land. Mission Trails Regional Park became a true asset to the community.

Recently, examination of historic maps and aerial photographs from the 1930s led me to two likely spots where gigantic oaks could be found just off the main park road which is "old" Mission Gorge Road. The two areas are where folks might picnic or party in the 1930s. And maybe where I had lunch forty years ago. Taking the short drive from Downtown San Diego to where Louise was found takes about fifteen minutes using surface streets. It would have taken a little longer in 1931 in a Model T or other period car on two-lane roads at night.

On April 21, 2021, exactly ninety years since the discovery of Louise's body, crime scene photographs and old maps in hand, I walked east off the paved road once known as Mission Gorge Road and now renamed Father Junipero Serra Trail. The well-used dusty trail winds into a grove of oak trees. To the north of the trail, a rocky escarpment favored by rock climbers juts upward. I ignored the obligatory STAY ON THE DEDICATED PATH and BEWARE OF RATTLESNAKES signs. In my mind, those admonitions clearly applied to other hikers, not someone trying to solve a terrible murder.

There, along the edges of a small drainage and a flat area ideal for picnicking, or making out, or for murder, stood a cluster of old oaks. Were any of them standing in 1931? How close was I to the spot that Antonio Martinez selected for his family's picnic nine decades ago? The answer was remarkably close indeed. While the exact oak tree, which might be more than one hundred thirty years old now, could not be located, I certainly was in the right area. Most likely, the oak pointed out by Cyril Smith to Thomas Jordan in the 1950s was destroyed in the construction of the "new" Mission Gorge Road. Hundreds of commuters pass over Louise's murder scene daily. If history is circular, as some philosophers say, the ovate Oak Grove Loop took me close to Louise.

Items Recovered from Crime Scenes

Artifacts of the Dead

Virginia Brooks
- Four public library books
- Burlap bags
- Flowered dress
- Reddish cloth coat
- Shoes and socks
- Leaves
- Two "Indian Head" nickels
- Scrap of bookbinding
- Orange-and-black handkerchief

Louise Teuber
- Knotted rope
- Pile of clothing
- Silk hose (on the body)
- Shoes (on the body)
- Purse (some distance from the hanging tree)
- Brassiere and panties (Newly purchased and never worn)
- Address book

Hazel Bradshaw
- Waltham wristwatch
- String of inexpensive beads
- Tan purse with compact and candy bar remnants
- Seventy-eight cents
- Print dress

- Silk coat
- Underclothing
- Pair of flats
- Hat

Author's Notes

As I was working on this book, giving presentations on the cases, and regaling almost anyone who would listen with the tragic stories, several persons asked me how I came across the idea for a true crime book set in the San Diego of the 1930s. Given my background as an archaeologist and anthropologist interested in local Native people, such an undertaking seemed a little out of my wheelhouse to many people. But not really. Anthropologists and, by extension, archaeologists, are trained to interpret human actions and cultures. Their data can include artifacts, burials, soils, patterns on the land, and, in the historic period, archival materials. From these bits and pieces of the past, archaeologists slip into their detective mode and tease out the meaning of their evidence.

Okay, but how did I get from ceramic sherds and arrow points to a noose, a missing bloodied knife, and burlap bags along a twisted trail of unsolved murders?

The unromantic answer is that over fifteen years ago, I was researching old San Diego newspapers for an entirely different story, albeit equally tragic in its own way—the removal of the Capitan Grande Kumeyaay from their traditional lands in Eastern San Diego County. There, splashed across the April 15, 1931, *San Diego Union* front page was a bold headline announcing the shocking discovery of Louise Teuber's semi-nude body in Mission Gorge. And so, the sinuous journey into murder and unserved justice began.

More recently, after reading the truly fine book *The Man from the Train* by Bill James and his daughter Rachel McCarthy James and being inspired by researching and potentially solving decades-old murders, I revisited some dusty files (both paper and floppy disc). My goal was to see if I could either solve some of the San Diego murders, or at least tell the story of the murdered angels. My surprise was palpable when I realized I had begun research on one murder over thirty years ago and at that time had a poorly written fifty-page first draft. The long and winding trail began decades ago with my research on the fascinating unsolved murder of the local dancer Fritzi Mann in 1924. But that is another story already covered in a short piece by local historian Rick Crawford in his excellent book *San Diego Yesterday* and in the true crime book *Murder at the Sea Cove Cottages* by James Stewart.

Over the years, one thing led to another, and soon, I had compiled information on several unsolved murders in San Diego between 1923 and 1935. I grew surprised by the sheer number of murders and suicides, or apparent suicides, in San Diego. What started as a single thin file folder of old newspaper articles copied from brittle microfilm on to slick gray copy paper grew to include death certificates, autopsy reports, court transcripts, communications with family members, old maps, internet downloads, and even family photographs (thank you, Diane Powe).

Not content with archival material alone, I visited the locations where the bodies were found, including several hikes through Mission Trails Regional Park, walked the route taken by Moss Garrison and Hazel Bradshaw, and even trespassed on federal property to view the Virginia Brooks crime scene. I stood in front of the Teuber and Bradshaw homes, and visited the gravesites of the unfortunate young women. Either by telephone, email, or through letters, I interviewed Diane Powe, the daughter of Herman Newby, Thomas Jordan, a friend of Cyril Smith who looms as a possible suspect in the murder of Louise Teuber, communicated with Craig Bradshaw, the nephew of Hazel Bradshaw, and others.

I would like to report that the San Diego Police Department showed interest in my research and allowed me access to notes and files from their investigations almost ninety years ago. No such luck. Hoping they would share information and if they still had evidence, maybe even allow for DNA testing of the rope that killed Louise Teuber, I filed two sets of requests under the California Public Records Act. In both cases, the response was that under California Code Section 6254(f), Investigatory Files will not be shared with the public if the notes and files "would endanger the successful completion of the investigation or a related investigation." The over-ninety-year-old information I requested could not be made available because the three cases were still open, although not-by-police-department-definition active. Really?

Pursuing that line of thought further, I directly contacted the San Diego Police Department. Lieutenant Dobbs, of the department, with no relation to the Dobbs family involved in the Bradshaw case, was gracious and professional in explaining the rules. Unless a case was officially closed, it simply was not police policy to share investigative materials with the public. Trying a different approach, I asked to be informed simply if the police or sheriff kept any evidence from the three murder cases. The official answer from the San Diego police was, "After a diligent search and reasonable inquiry, the San Diego Police Department has determined it has no responsive records."

The San Diego Sheriff's Department was much more helpful. Their cold case unit possesses literally hundreds of cardboard boxes containing files and records going back to the 1930s. According to Sergeant Tim Chantler of the Homicide and Cold Case Department, his office does have files for both the Brooks and Teuber cases. Lieutenant Lisa

Brannan is, as of this writing, extremely interested in the Teuber case and hopes that the Sheriff's Department will release non-sensitive documents for both the Brooks and Teuber cases. As of late August 2023, the sheriff's legal department is reviewing my request for release of the files for review. They have indicated they may release redacted records in the near future.

And there you have it. Dead girls. Dead records.

I grew up in San Diego and am intimately familiar with all the scenes and places where the murders took place or where a body was found, and where the young women lived their brief lives. Thinking back on my childhood in San Diego of the mid-to-late 1960s, I realized that essentially only a generation had passed since the murders of the 1930s.

In my youth, many of the persons affected by the murders were still alive—I might have passed them on the street or ridden the Number 7 bus with them traveling down Park Boulevard past where Hazel Bradshaw met her end. I certainly had walked past Louise Teuber's home on Vermont Street and hiked Black (Cowles) Mountain in Mission Trails Regional Park where her nearly naked body swung suspended by a rope. Like Virginia Brooks' brother, Gordon, I had pedaled my Schwinn bicycle up and down University Avenue. More to the point, one of the murderers who took a young life could have been my neighbor, the guy who pumped gas on the top of Texas Street (yes, in California, attendants used to check your oil and pump your gas) Or he may have been the strange man in the long coat, leering at young women who hung around the North Park Theatre on University Avenue, where Louise and Myrtle used to go.

In writing this book, I hope that to some extent, the murdered young women, who will eternally be youthful and full of vigor, have been brought back to life. In a different scenario, little Virginia would grow up and live well into the

1990s, having experienced the tumultuous sixties, a man on the moon, and the pages of history flashing by. Given her penchant for reading, perhaps she would have become an author or a literature professor. Her two brothers would not have had to grieve for her. Perhaps her distraught mother would not have died from a botched abortion.

Instead of a gruesome death in a lonely oak grove, restless Louise might have left dull San Diego and made it to Chicago. She could have become a part of that city's vibrant history and culture, maybe even attending the 1933 Chicago World's Fair, purchasing one of the thirty-nine million admissions. Celebrating what was termed a "Century of Progress," Louise might have roller skated or danced at one of the brightly lit pavilions at the fair. Her diary may have chronicled the exciting new young men she dated. Hazel Bradshaw and Moss might have continued their relationship, gone to even more movies, maybe even gotten married, and if not, there was a line of suitors to take his place.

In my mind, as well as in photographs splashed across the front pages of old newspapers, I see Virginia, Louise, and Hazel almost daily. To paraphrase another author, everywhere I look, images of the unfortunate young women in these stories seem to materialize. Sometimes the images are crystal clear. At other times, they are gauzy. Regardless, I hope they have also become real to you.

ACKNOWLEDGMENTS

This is where the author admits that without help from a wide variety of people, this book would not have been possible. I think that for nonfiction works that admission is particularly true, given the factual rather than creative fictional nature of the genre. The events and main characters in this book are not a fictive creation of my sometimes overly imaginative mind. They lived, and maybe more importantly, died. Died too soon. True crime is a subgenre of nonfiction, or perhaps, as some argue, its own genre. Regardless. I may have knitted these stories together but the blood, guts, and people who inhabit them appeared not from a fertile mind. Today, they reside in archives, interviews, photographs, and all of the ephemera left by people's life on this Earth (no matter how short that life may have been).

For research that led to this book, the greatest debt is to Nancy Drew (otherwise known as my daughter Cris Eide). Cris possesses a dogged posture when it comes to research. Her skills extended far and wide across the archival world. Cris also made the trek to local cemeteries to provide gravesite photographs for some of our characters. Katy Phillips, archivist at the San Diego History Center opened several avenues of research for me including several of the evocative photographs used in this book. Over the years Rick Crawford first at the old San Diego Historical Society (now the History Center) and later at the San Diego Public Library California Room was always a great source of San Diego facts and trivia. Institutional facilities include the

Bancroft Library at the University of California—Berkeley, Special Collections at the University of Southern California, and the Records Department at San Diego Superior Court all house materials used in this book.

Dr. Madeleine Hinkes, a noted forensic anthropologist, helped me with the wonders of the human digestive tract, death by oral copulation, and the vagaries of rigor mortis. Attorney Alan Ridenour clarified several points of law for me, often with a pint or two of beer to lubricate our minds. To find the oak grove where Louise Teuber was hanged, Fred Kramer, a volunteer park ranger at Mission Trails Regional Park measured and studied oak trees in the park. He also correctly suggested that the murder site was probably underneath present-day Mission Gorge Road. Deputy Sheriff Tim Chantler and Lt. Lisa Brannan did all that they could to share official records with me.

When the book was nearly complete, Mr. Thomas Jordan, a ninety-three-year-old gentleman contacted me after the *San Diego Reader* printed an excerpt from the Louise Teuber chapters. Much to my surprise and joy, Mr. Jordan knew Cyril Smith, one of Teuber's boyfriends. It was Mr. Jordan who gave me new, first-hand information, on Smith, including his weak alibi for the night of the murder, his supposed sexual relations with Louise, and the statement that she had choked to death performing oral sex.

While reserving for myself any factual or editorial errors in this book, my wife Lisa Carrico saw this tome through several drafts and redrafts. My longtime colleague in the environmental field, Tom Larkin, and Jennifer Redmond, my ex-editor at Sunbelt Publications, took long looks at the manuscript when, realistically, it was not ready for their critical professional eyes. Hopefully, for the three of you, there are enough commas appropriately placed herein. And of course, the staff of WildBlue including Steve Jackson, Michael Cordova, Stephanie Johnson Lawson, Jazzminn Morecraft, Elijah Toten, and Jenn Waterman. Thank you.

Bibliography

NEWSPAPERS
Danville Virginia Bee
Greenfield Indiana Daily Reporter
Hancock Indiana Democrat
Los Angeles Express
Los Angeles Times
Madera Tribune
Miami Florida News
Minneapolis Standard Examiner
Modesto News-Herald
National City Star News
Oakland Tribune
Pomona Progress Report
Sacramento Bee
San Diego Sun
San Diego Union
San Diego Evening Tribune
San Francisco Examiner
Times Advocate Escondido

BOOKS/MANUSCRIPTS/JOURNALS

James, Bill and Rachel McCarthy James. *The Man from the Train: The Solving of a Century-Old Serial Killer Mystery.* 2017

Hinkes, Madeline Forensic Anthropology. In: *Practical Cold Case Homicide Investigations Procedural Manual.*

Richard H. Walton (ed.). CRC Press: New York, 2014.

Shurman-Kauflin, Deborah. https://www.psychologytoday.com/us/blog/disturbed/201402/does-criminal-profiling-work

Schuler, Kelly. Scrapbook from his time as San Diego coroner. San Diego History Center.

Lamb, Molly. *Aborted Justice: The Hazel Bradshaw Investigation.* Manuscript on file at the San Diego History Center.

Sample, Lisa. *The Social Construction of the Sex Offender.* Doctoral dissertation. University of Missouri-Saint Louis, 2001.

Sample, Lisa. An Examination of the Degree to Which Sexual Offenders Kill. *Criminal Justice Review*, 2006.

Walsh, Anthony and Craig Hemmens. Introduction to Criminology. Sage Publications: London, 2019.

INSTITUTIONS/ARCHIVAL SOURCES

Ancestry.com

California Voter Registrations 1920-1950

Colby, Dr. Elliot G., "Death Certificate." May 11, 1931

Draft Registration Cards 195-1940

Gunn, Chester. "Autopsy: Number 31-016980," February 11, 1931

Indiana State Board of Health, Division of Vital Statistics.

San Diego City Directories 1920-1940

San Diego City Planning Department

San Diego City Schools District

San Diego County Clerk's Office

San Diego County Medical Examiner's Office

San Diego History Center

San Diego Police Department

San Diego Public Library, Central Branch

San Diego Sheriff's Department

San Diego Superior Court Central Records

San Diego Telephone Directories 1925-1935

State of Washington Marriage Records 1854-2013

Toomey, Dr. F.E. "Death Certificate." April 28, 1931

United States Federal Census 1900, 1920, 1930, 1940

United State Geological Survey Topographical Maps (Point Loma, La Mesa, National City, La Jolla)

United States National Cemetery Interment Control Forms

University of California, Berkely. Bancroft Library

University of Southern California Regional History Collections

INTERVIEWS

William Bacon (Son of Loretta Orthick (Bacon) friend of Louise Teuber)

Lt. Lisa Bannan Homicide Team II & Cold Cases, San Diego Sheriff's Department

Craig Bradshaw (Nephew of Hazel Bradshaw)

Lt. Tim Chantler Homicide Team II & Cold Cases, San Diego Sheriff's Department

Lt. Matt Dobbs San Diego Police Homicide Unit

Madeliene Hinkes (Forensic anthropologist San Diego County Medical Examiner's Office)

Thomas Jordan (Ex-Student and colleague of Cyril Smith)

David Lewis (Julian Historic Society)

Donna Starr Lewis (Long time Julian resident)

Rowena Lux (Niece of Virginia Brooks)

Katy Phillips (Archivist San Diego History Center)

Diane Powe (Daughter of Herman Newby)

For More News About Richard Carrico,
Signup For Our Newsletter:

http://wbp.bz/newsletter

Word-of-mouth is critical to an author's long-term success. If you appreciated this book please leave a review on the Amazon sales page:

https://wbp.bz/motl

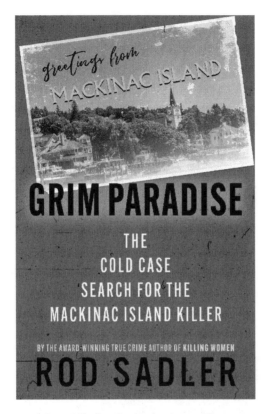

ALSO AVAILABLE FROM JAMES STEWART AND WILDBLUE PRESS!

https://wbp.bz/blueseacottagea

This "fast-paced, thoughtful true-crime" examines the cultural shifts of Jazz Age America through a beautiful dancer's mysterious and scandalous death (Kirkus, starred review).

Made in the USA
Las Vegas, NV
25 November 2023

81494891R00120